Sounding

CW01401917

Issue 13

These
Sporting
Times

EDITORS
Stuart Hall
Doreen Massey
Michael Rustin

GUEST EDITOR
Andrew Blake

POETRY EDITOR
Carole Satyamurti

REVIEWS EDITORS
Becky Hall and
Susanna Rustin

ART EDITOR
Tim Davison

EDITORIAL OFFICE
Lawrence & Wishart
99a Wallis Road
London E9 5LN

MARKETING CONSULTANT
Mark Perryman

Soundings is published three
times a year, in autumn,
spring and summer by:
Soundings Ltd
c/o Lawrence & Wishart
99a Wallis Road
London E9 5LN

ADVERTISEMENTS
Write for information to Soundings,
c/o Lawrence & Wishart

SUBSCRIPTIONS
1999 subscription rates are (for three issues):
UK: Institutions £70, Individuals £35
Rest of the world: Institutions £80, Individuals
£45

Collection as a whole © Soundings 1999
Individual articles © the authors 1999

ISSN 1362 6620
ISBN 0 85315 920 3

Text setting Art Services, Norwich
Cover photograph: © Sarah Williams

Printed in Great Britain by
Cambridge University Press, Cambridge

CONTENTS

———————————— *Continued on next page* ————————————

Continued from previous page

NOTES ON CONTRIBUTORS

Geoffrey Adkins (1941-1997) was editor of Limestone publications. He published several volumes of poetry, including *A Difficult Peace* (Ceolfrith Press, 1982). He worked in adult education in London.

Geoff Andrews is Senior Lecturer in Politics at the University of Hertfordshire, and an Associate Lecturer at The Open University. He is co-editor of *New Left, New Right and Beyond: Taking the Sixties Seriously*, (1999) and *Ruskin College: Contesting Knowledge, Dissenting Politics* (1999).

Andrew Blake is Professor and Head of Cultural Studies at King Alfred's College, Winchester. His latest book is the edited collection *Living Through Pop* (Routledge 1999).

Adam Brown is a Research fellow at the Manchester Institute for Popular Culture, Manchester Metropolitan University, and a member of the Government's Football Task Force. He is joint author with Andy Walsh of *Not For Sale: Manchester United, Murdoch and the Defeat of BSkyB*, published by Mainstream Press in October 1999.

Gemma Bryden started training as a kickboxer in 1996, and won both the NAK national championship at under 60KG class, and silver medal at the AMA British Open championship at under 50KG class, in 1998.

Simon Cook is a computer consultant who recently moved to Paris, where he lives and works.

Susanne Ehrhardt grew up in Germany and now lives in England. A selection of her poems was published in *New Chatto Poets II*.

Steve Greenfield and Guy Osborn are joint directors of the MA in Law and Popular Culture at the University of Westminster. Their book on football is to be published by Pluto.

Fred Halliday teaches International relations at LSE. His books include *Islam and the Myth of Confrontation* and *Religion in the Middle East*. Both have been translated into Turkish. His most recent book is *Revolution and World Politics: The Rise and Fall of the Sixth Great Power*.

Steve Hawes worked in sports and music journalism at Granada Television during the 1960s. He is currently Head of Community and Performing Arts at King Alfred's College, Winchester.

Nick Henry is a Lecturer in Economic Geography at the University of Birmingham with a particular interest in globalisation and regional development.

Judith Kazantzis's *Selected Poems* was published by Sinclair Stevenson in 1995, and *Swimming Through the Grand Hotel* by Enitharmon in 1997. Her most recent book is *The Odysseus Poems: Fictions on the Odyssey of Homer*.

Cherron Lee Johnson is currently completing her MA in Design and Media Arts at the University of Westminster.

Robin Leanse works in London, where he lives with his five sons.

Alastair Loadman teaches Sports Studies at King Alfred's College, Winchester.

Adam Locks is a doctoral student at King Alfred's College, Winchester.

Angela McRobbie is Professor of Communications at Goldsmiths College London and author of *British Fashion Design* (1998) and *In the Culture Society* (1999).

Adrian Passmore is an urban geographer and resident of Birmingham. Recently, he has been a temporary resident of Berlin studying the city's transformation following the fall of the wall.

Alyson Pendlebury is based at the Department of English, University of Southampton, where she is working towards her doctorate, on the subject of Fictions of Jewish Identity in First World War Britain.

Jonathan Rutherford is part of the Signs of the Times group. His latest book is *I Am No Longer Myself Without You: An Anatomy of Love* (1999). He is co-author, with Jeremy Gilbert, of the SOTT pamphlet, *Balancing Acts*.

Carol Smith teaches American Studies at King Alfred's College, Winchester. She is joint author, with Jude Davies, of *Gender, Ethnicity and Sexuality in American Film* (1997).

Alan Tomlinson is Professor of Sport and Leisure Cultures at the University of Brighton. His book *Sport and Leisure Cultures - Local, National and Global Dimensions* is published by University of Minnesota Press.

Andy Wallis works at King Alfred's College, Winchester. His doctoral project is on space, cyberspace and technologies of surveillance.

Gregory Warren Wilson is a professional violinist. His poetry has won many awards. His latest collection is *Hanging Windchimes in a Vacuum* (1997).

The lessons of Kosovo

The editors of *Soundings*, like many on the left in Britain, did not find it easy to make a straightforward response, either sympathetic or hostile, to the NATO intervention in the Balkans War.[1] Some of us thought that there was a humanitarian case for armed intervention, comparable to that which had justified the Vietnamese intervention against Pol Pot's Cambodian regime, or Tanzania's against Idi Amin's Uganda, and which would and should have justified intervention to halt the Rwandan genocide had it taken place. It is the moral responsibility, as Michael Walzer has argued, of bystanders, whoever they are, to intervene to prevent atrocity where they can. Once the mass expulsions of the Kosovans, and the military intervention against Serbia, were both in full process, it seemed to us difficult to argue that the preferred outcome was a victory for Milosovic, which is what an anti-war position would at that time, though perhaps not at an earlier stage before the bombing started, have amounted to.

But how had this whole disaster come about? Was the undoubted humanitarian crisis which was used to justify NATO's intervention its actual cause, or its mere pretext? Had NATO first decided to 'teach Milosovic a lesson', following the humiliation of the UN during the Bosnian crisis, and to impose the dominance of NATO as the single global military force, as its objectives? Was it possible that the fate of the Kosovans at the hands of the Serbs was not merely a political bonus to NATO commanders, giving much-needed public

---

1. This editorial was written following a discussion of these issues at a *Soundings* contributors meeting in July, in which different views were explored. Subscribers interested in attending these quarterly discussions are invited to write to the *Soundings* office for details.

Soundings

justification for their war, but had been calculated as such, as the predicted and predictable response of Milosovic to the NATO bombing campaign?

It is difficult to answer these questions with certitude. It seems likely, however, that political misjudgement (Milosovic had given way quickly when air power had been eventually deployed in Bosnia) and expediency (constraining what kinds of military intervention were deemed politically acceptable) played as much part as informed strategic calculation in what took place. We can say now that NATO's armed intervention brought about the very catastrophe it was intended to prevent (terror and mass expulsions in Kosovo). One can say too that this consequence should have been anticipated, to some degree. But this is different from asserting that everything took place according to a script written beforehand in Washington and London. What is certain is that armed violence is always unpredictable in its effects, and usually develops a cumulatively destructive momentum of its own. The intervention in Kosovo has so far solved few problems in this region, and at great human cost. We recoiled in particular at the idea of a supposedly humanitarian war in which Western and in particular American casualties were weighed in value on a scale of one to a thousand or more of casualties among former Yugoslavs. It seemed to us that the responsibility of politicians is to protect and spare all human lives, not merely the lives of their own political subjects, and the contrary of this seemed to us to be approaching a kind of racism, which was all the more unacceptable wearing its 'humanitarian' face. This is not to ignore the fact that in this war, unlike in the war against Iraq, avoiding unnecessary casualties even among 'the enemy' was in reality given an unusual priority. But if risks have to be run, to prevent atrocity, it cannot be right that virtually none of these risks are to the subjects of the intervening powers.

And what about the manifest double standards employed by NATO in this as in virtually all of its military interventions? Why had injustices to Kurds or Palestinians been ignored for decades, and a blind eye turned to genocide in Rwanda, but here, on Western Europe's doorstep, synthetic moral outrage and a vast military machine were mobilised? Why was it only now that the problem of Kosovo was recognised, when its dangerous potential had been clear during the Bosnian crisis? We came to see that in the era of global communications and human international rights, moral claims had become a significant factor, but rarely the decisive one, in decision-making about political and military action.

The Falklands War depended both on the claims to self-determination of the British Falkland Islanders, *and* on Britain's continuing imperial ambitions; Kuwait was defended *both* because of its international entitlements as a sovereign state, *and* because of its strategic importance as an oil state; the Kosovans were defended *both* because of the injuries done to them, *and* because of Western determination to defeat Serbian (and less directly, Russian), ambitions, in the Balkans region. Justifications of moral legitimacy seem to have become one condition, but by no means a sufficient or determining one, of the West's recent military interventions.

It is something positive, perhaps, that the claims of 'human rights' may now count at least for something more than they used to in international relations. The pending extradition of General Pinochet is another straw in the wind here. But we would be gullible if we mistook our governments' rhetorical posturing on these questions for the full explanation of why they acted as they did. The crisis in East Timor, unfolding as this article is written, is revealing these levels of hypocrisy in a terrible way. Just as one might have imagined that Kosovo represented at least some process of learning from the disasters of Bosnia and Rwanda, we observe that after all nothing may have changed. It seems that decades of complicity with the authoritarian rulers of Indonesia are not going to be set aside because of a democratic vote in a small country, least of all to preserve the reputation of the United Nations. In the light of these events, the UN appears to have been brushed aside in Kosovo not merely because of the practical necessities of urgent action, as was then claimed, but also because the United States and British governments see its power as a rival to their own, and positively desire its impotence.[2]

What is really needed in this situation is to get beneath the surface of events - to which, like everyone else, we had our sometimes confused day-by-day responses - to try to find an understanding of what was fundamentally at issue in the Balkans Crisis. Here there continues to be a massive failure of Western imagination and understanding in regard to the problems created by the collapse of Communism in Russia and Eastern Europe. The major culpability of the West in this region does not lie in the specifics of the Kosovan,

---

2   We will of course be relieved if by the time this issue appears, this assessment comes to seem too harsh.

or of the preceding Bosnian crisis, but in its short-sighted and exploitative response to the collapse of this rival political system in its entirety. In this respect, the problems of the former Yugoslavia are a microcosm of the much larger disaster which has befallen the former Soviet Union, partly as a result of the misguided and ideologically driven nature of Western interventions.

The underlying problem in Yugoslavia was plainly what was to happen after the collapse of Communism. What possible pathways were available to bring this former nation, or its component nations, from the partial version of 'modernisation' which they had accomplished, with considerable success, under Communist governments since 1945, into a post-Communist era? It should have been possible to foresee the dangers that would be posed, both in the Soviet Union and Yugoslavia, by latent nationalisms. These were especially acute in the Balkans, the permanent border-country of the successive competing empires of the Hapsburgs, the Ottomans, the Russians, and the Nazis, with other powers like Britain and France always eager to put in their spoke. In this region, there were no stable equations between ethnic and religious cultures and political jurisdictions. The 'normal' course of modernisation, described by Ernest Gellner, in which a unified national culture developed in many territories in the nineteenth and twentieth centuries, as a container for industrialisation, had been pre-empted by the complex imperial history of this region. The main task was always going to be to find a system of political containment for the nationalist forces which were otherwise certain to fill the vacuum left by the collapse of the Communist system. It was an achievement of Communism that ethnic divisions were contained for so long, in the former Yugoslavia and USSR, just as the Communist Party of South Africa deserves credit for its contribution to the non-racial universalism of the African National Congress.

It is not as if this problem should have been so difficult for the Western European or United States governments to understand. European integration in the post-war period had been undertaken, with assistance from the Americans and their Marshall Plan, in response to a parallel problem. This was how to contain potential nationalist antagonisms after the defeat of Nazi Germany at the end of the Second World War; and the Franco-German alliance and the European Union was the wise solution to this. It is worth remembering, however, that this solution had been discovered fifty years too late, following the disastrous failure of a pro-nationalist model of development after Germany's earlier defeat in 1918. Nationalism after 1918 took both an idealised and sanctified form as the doctrine of national self-determination, influential in the Versailles Treaty; it took its catastrophic turn under the Nazis. It then led to global disaster.

And lo and behold, it is exactly this '1918, nations-first model' that the West chose to espouse for its defeated eastern rival after 1989. Having in 1945 decided in its own heartland to learn the lessons of 1918, it has opted in the former Eastern Europe to repeat its pro-nationalist errors of the inter-war period. In the former Soviet Union, Yeltsin's dissolution of the Soviet Union in favour of its component nationalities was welcomed as a fatal blow against the still suspiciously reform-Communist Gorbachev. The result of this, and of the imposition of free market ideology on a system and political culture quite unsuited to it, has been disastrous, culminating in economic chaos and in the rule over Russia by thieves.

In the former Yugoslavia, Slovenia's and then Croatia's exit from the Federation were encouraged and welcomed by their respective Western protectors, Austria and Germany. Whilst ostensibly the war in Kosovo was fought to secure multi-ethnic coexistence, and the restoration of the former autonomy of the province within the remains of federal Yugoslavia, it seems likely that its effect will be to reinforce ethnic particularism. The Kosovan Liberation Army, a factor in provoking Serbian oppression in the first instance, may well prove to be the ultimate inheritors of power in Kosovo as a result of the war. The logic of the nationalist politics encouraged, intentionally or otherwise, by the West is such that the KLA are now engaged in meting out to the remaining Serbs the same treatment as that to which the Kosovan Albanians were subjected by Serbian paramilitaries. It is not clear what will now obstruct the emergence of a Kosovan Albanian State, viable or otherwise, even though the West did not and still does not support this. There now seems more to be said for the idea of a partition of Kosovo, guaranteed by Russia as well as the West, than there did at the outset or even during the war.

It is remarkable that Western politicians should have been sponsoring self-determination east of their own borders, at a time when they had decided that supra-national forms of integration or containment were the necessary pathway to full modernity within their own boundaries. They had become adept, in

Catalonia, Scotland, even perhaps Northern Ireland, in making use of larger structures of containment and identification as ways of releasing intra-national pressures, and allowing a necessary measure of autonomy and self-expression to nationalist currents inside their own states. Yet in the former Eastern Europe, such remaining structures as there were have been utterly cast aside. The selective inclusion of some favoured states in the charmed circle of the European Union and NATO (Hungary, the Czech Republic, Poland) has only worsened the plight of those left out. It seems that a continuing preoccupation with the ideological struggle against residues of Communism is what explains this folly, just as fears of the Bolshevik revolution played a large part in unhinging the West's political sense in the inter-war period.

Milosovic has thus only attempted to write his own part in a larger play already scripted for him by the covertly pro-nationalist Western response to the crisis of Yugoslavia. States use the resources available to them. The principal military resource available to Milosovic was the former Yugoslav army, and his principal political resource has been ethnic absolutism. Nationalism based on military power was hardly an option without a precedent - it had been, after all, the essence of Prussia's unification of Germany in the previous century. The Yugoslav tragedy is that the failed 'partial modernisation' of Communism was followed by utter anachronism, by a Serbian strategy of military nationalism embarked on at the very moment when the nation-state elsewhere is in terminal decline as the facilitator or container of modern social development. The West has been confused and myopic in its response to this situation, on the one hand condoning the erosion of the remaining structures of containment (the Yugoslav Federation), on the other vainly trying to secure continued 'multi-ethnic co-operation' (in Bosnia or Kosovo).

The West has chosen, in its public response to Milosovic's adventures, to deal largely in the moralistic terms of personal demonisation. It is a notable fact of Western politics today that the binary structures of ideological antagonism which maintained its internal unity and purpose throughout the Cold War have been transmuted into such personalised hatreds of individualised enemies, wherever and whenever it encounters the limits of its power. But this denunciatory rhetoric obscures far more than it reveals. The scale of death and injury inflicted by the economic catastrophe of the former Soviet Union, following the West's triumph over it; or by NATO's continuing economic sanctions on Iraq; or by the continuing failure of Western promises to bring investment and prosperity to the new South Africa, or to the Palestinians, provide little basis for western moral self-righteousness. Unfortunately, the mass sufferings of poverty are less visible, and less attributable to their causes, than the personalised misdeeds of individuals. The global media currency which gives a 'value' to humanitarian crises where individual victims can be photographed and interviewed, also prefers to hold individual leaders rather than less visible social processes responsible for ills and harms.

There have been the glimmerings of enlightenment in the proposals of some European politicians (initially, Joschka Fischer, the German Green Foreign Minister) for the economic reconstruction of the Balkans and its eventual admission to the European Union. This at least recognises the need for a post-national structure, on a scale which can nurture economic and social development, which can impose rules of reasonable democratic practice, and which can provide guarantees for minorities which preclude the necessity for strategies of desperate self-defence and self-assertion. The European Union is, unlike NATO, an institution based on formulated principles of democratic practice, and respect for human rights (and of course the market economy); and its extension and development into this region are thus to be cautiously welcomed. There is no decent future for independent states derived from the former Yugoslavia without their inclusion in some broader containing federation. The pity is that this recognition by the European Union has come only now, after two terrible wars and after hundreds of thousands of people have been expelled from their homes. But this is the only hopeful development that has emerged from this crisis. It is vital that something substantial should now come out of it.

M R

New Left and New Labour

Modernisation or a new modernity?

Geoff Andrews

Geoff Andrews *looks at New Labour's identification of modernity with managerialism and argues that the New Left tradition offers more hopeful approaches.*

Recent attempts to understand the provenance of New Labour, as well as arguments over its underlying dynamics, its political orientation and its future prospects, have made connections - not all of them accurate - with the traditions of the New Left. The main point of comparison is the primacy given to modernisation as the organising framework - indeed raison d'être - for New Labour's entire existence. From its inception New Labour has shared with the New Left the need to break free from labourism, to resituate its 'project' within the fundamental changes characteristic of late modern societies, notably the need to come to terms with globalisation, the restructuring of work and family life and the implications of technological shifts. This links it in particular with *Marxism Today's* 'new times' analysis, where many of these developments were seen to herald a whole set of new political 'settlements'. Indeed, for many, *Marxism Today* was the leading intellectual influence on New Labour. For Jonathan Freedland, the former had a 'parental' role in shaping the upbringing and development of the latter (*Guardian*, 9.9.98), while Stuart Hall has acknowledged that Blair was the 'Marxism *Today* candidate' (*New Statesman*, 5.12.97). For more vigorous sympathisers of the current government such as Democratic Left (DL), there is a relatively clear and unambiguous line of continuity between 'new times' and the Blair agenda. Moreover DL's recent adoption of the term 'modernising left' - 'on-side, but not always on message' - has reinforced this connection, as well as delineating the political boundaries between those 'modernisers' who accept in principle the main elements of New Labour's programme, and those 'traditionalists' who still cling to the past. The trouble here, of course, is that 'modernisation' and 'New Labour' remain synonymous; the space in which to articulate an alternative view of modernity becomes increasingly difficult to find. Such a task, however, which this journal in particular has set itself, will become more important as the faultlines emerge.

It is not only the *Marxism Today* heritage - what I have called the third moment of the New Left - that has been associated with the development of New Labour modernisation.[1] More general similarities have been observed, in the common concern of New Labour and their New Left predecessors with the role of intellectuals, the need for long-term strategy, and the turn towards civil society rather than the state for solutions. For many, greater liberalisation and multi-culturalism is seen as the realisation of the liberal values of the 1960s, while the need to democratise and modernise state institutions also has its origins in the earlier New Left political generations. In one of the most interesting arguments in this respect, Michael Kenny suggested in this magazine three years ago (*Soundings* 4) that Blair's attempt to depart from Labourism mirrored in many ways features of New Left anti-statism, particularly through attempts for renewal through a deeper and more energetic engagement with the movements and currents in civil society. He traced the development of similar positions through the New Left thinkers, Charter 88 supporters, *Marxism Today* and the SDP, to New Labour's commitment to 'reconnect the party to the energies and aspirations of groups beyond its boundaries'. What these currents had in common, he argued, was 'the conviction that Labour had lost touch with the real story of British fortunes in the post-war period - including the relative decline of its industrial performance, and the impact of important social changes which

---

1. See 'The Three New Lefts and Their Legacies', in G. Andrews et al (eds), *New Left, New Right and Beyond: Taking the Sixties Seriously*, Macmillan 1999.

were producing identities and concerns within the social arena from which the party remained aloof'. The concept of civil society was pivotal in the realisation of the New Left legacy in New Labour's reformulation of a radical programme. This included (he suggested), movements partly defined by a more 'diversified' concept of 'the political', to include 'the everyday, the emotional and the non-human environment'. The implications for policy were clear in aspects of constitutional reform, alternative ways of providing public services and more 'post-materialist' initiatives.

Kenny was writing six months or so before the election of the Blair government - a more optimistic period for many of us. His warnings at the time included the danger of the 'partnership' model 'displacing tough questions about social rights, obligations and duties on to communities which do not have the slightest chance of tackling them, without external resources and co-operation'. He also warned of the pitfalls of reverting to an uncritical acceptance of the globalisation thesis and conservative communitarian positions.

We can see two years on that these concerns, in essence about the distribution of power, and inequality between social groups, have become major faultlines in the New Labour approach. Increasingly, New Labour's version of modernisation, as it begins to unfold, appears as a conservative one. It is a top-down version, driven by new managerialist ideology, and acceptance of neo-liberal discourses of globalisation; at times it appeals as 'bottom-up', but only in populist ways, addressing its social constituencies in the language of customers or as individuals, with an unlimited capacity to achieve, if they 'work hard and play by the rules'.[2] This sets it apart from the more critical engagement with modernity characteristic of the New Left. And this means that analogies between the two, however useful at a general level, are much more problematic, when the 'meta' political questions of class, power and structural inequality are raised. Indeed it is my argument here that the recent search for similarities is rather less useful than retaining the legacy of the New Left as an important source of critique of current government direction. Reconnecting in a creative way with the core of New Left traditions offers an alternative rather than complementary interpretation of modernisation.

What unified the New Left in its different guises was its critical interrogation

2.   R. Liddle and P. Mandelson, *The Blair Revolution*, Faber 1996.

of the effects of capitalist modernisation, as the pre-requisite for creating the conditions for a more democratic, pluralist and libertarian socialism. A re-reading of the *May Day Manifesto*, for example (written at a similar point in the second Wilson government to the current time), finds some striking parallels with our own situation. In the section entitled 'The Meaning of Modernization', it argued that beneath the Wilsonite rhetoric of the 'New Britain', the discourse of modernisation opened up a perspective of change, but at the same time mystified the process and set limits to it:

> Attitudes, habits, techniques, practices must change: the system of economic and social power, however, remains unchanged... Any discussion of long-term purposes is made to seem utopian, in the down-to-earth, pragmatic climate which modernization generates. The discussion about 'modernized Britain' is not about what sort of society, qualitatively, is being aimed at, but simply about how modernization is to be achieved. All programmes and perspectives are treated instrumentally. As a model of social change, modernization crudely foreshortens the historical development of society. Modernization is the ideology of the never-ending present. The whole past belongs to 'traditional' society and modernization is a technical means for breaking with the past, without creating a future. All is now: restless, visionless, faithless: human society diminished to a passing technique. No concentration of power, values or interests, no choice between competing priorities, is envisaged or encouraged. It is a technocratic model of society, conflict-free and politically neutral, dissolving genuine social conflicts ... Modernization presumes that no group in the society will be called upon to bear the costs of the scientific revolution - as if all men (sic) have an equal chance in shaping up the consensus, or as if, by some process of natural law, we all benefit equally from a rise in productivity. 'Modernization' is thus a way of masking what the real costs would be of creating in Britain a truly modern society'. [3]

The Manifesto For New Times, written over twenty years later, adopts a similar starting-point, describing the 'enormous inequalities in income, wealth and power, with key decisions taken by a minority of international financiers and

---

3. R. Williams et al (eds), *May Day Manifesto*, Penguin 1968 p45.

industrialists'.[4] The transformations it described - those associated with post-fordism, globalisation and technological change - produced 'new settlements', new 'sites of struggle', around which politics would come to be organised. It too warned of the social and economic costs of modernisation, which 'is promoting far more savage forms of social polarisation' (p34). It remained critical of the view that progressive change would emerge without any need for political and social struggle. In 'modernising' itself, the left must find a new 'division of labour between social movements and political parties, in mobilising people, expressing aspirations, challenging power and enacting change' (p364). A key question was 'on whose terms will this new era be moulded? (p36)'. The answer to this was to be found, of course, in the conflict of interests between 'progressive social forces' and big business - and there was a need to distinguish between 'conservative modernisation' and 'an alternative path to modernisation', based on humane, democratic and sustainable values.

Modernisation as managerialism

New Labour, in contrast to these perspectives, has a concept of modernity which appears one-dimensional, carrying all before it. It is its uncritical relationship to technocracy and managerialism that marks it out most from the New Left. It is not only the absence of a critique of the limits of managerialism that is important, but also the close parallels between New Labour's outlook and the underlying ethos of new managerialism. New Labour shares with new managerialism the obsession with achieving outcomes at the micro-level, on the principle of 'what matters is what works', where 'delivery, delivery, delivery' is the name of the game. Here, in place of ideology there is a 'can-do pragmatism' whereby sociological shifts act as the precursor to policy adaptation.[5] Alan Finlayson, in a recent *Political Quarterly* article (Spring 1999), has argued that it is this Demos liking for 'policy pragmatism', as opposed to the Gramscian meta-political critique of the economic and social system, which is the 'new times' legacy that lives on most in New Labour (p271).

At another level New Labour imbibes the new managerialist concepts of

4. 'Manifesto For New Times', quoted in S. Hall and M. Jacques (eds), *New Times*, Lawrence and Wishart 1989, p23.
5. A. Barnett, 'Corporate Control', *Prospect*, February 1999 p26; M. White, *Guardian* 29.7.99.

'empowerment', where individuals, through the development of social and human capital, are 'invested in' and offered various forms of 'inclusion'. Anthony Barnett has used the concept 'corporate populism' to describe the way Downing Street treats the Government of the country: 'It manages Party, Cabinet and Civil Service as if they were parts of a single giant company whose aim is to persuade voters that they are happy customers who want to return Labour to office' ('Corporate Control', p27). The latest Annual Report, available from Tescos, confirms further this analogy of delivering outcomes and satisfying customers. The managerialism now seems to overlap with all aspects of the Government's outlook; one of the purposes of 'enabling government', according to Blair himself, is to 'help families and communities improve their own performance'.[6] The problem here, as Wendy Wheeler has pointed out in A *New Modernity?*, is that 'Social relations can be loosely facilitated in any number of ways (good housing, full employment, for example), but they cannot be managed'.[7]

A key aspect of the new managerialism is the elimination of conflict and the re-building of employee-employer harmony. The third way is derived from similar principles, and sees the end of adversarial politics,[8] and the possibility of an all-inclusive society, based on building 'trust' at the micro-level and an 'enabling government' facilitating social partnerships at the macro-level. Where the New Left has always sought the 'systemic' context, and the sphere of meta-politics in which to situate its critique, New Labour by contrast looks to the micro, and has an unfailing belief in the possibilities of personal agency as the way out of 'exclusion'. Indeed the concept of a 'system' itself is anathema to them. Peter Mandelson found Anthony Barnett's proposal to project Charter 88's demands as a new system of government as 'sounding like Grosvenor Square' ('Corporate Control', p25).

Managers versus intellectuals

The different stories of modernity on offer are exemplified further by the contrast between the leading political players; the agents, mediators or

---

6. T. Blair, *The Third Way*, Fabian Society 1998.
7. W. Wheeler, A *New Modernity?*, Lawrence and Wishart 1999, p110.
8. See Chantal Mouffe, 'The Radical Centre: A Politics Without Adversary', *Soundings* 9, summer 1998.

facilitators of modernisation. For the New Left it was the new concept of the 'organic intellectual' that was crucial. Here, the more public and political role of the intellectual as social critic was crucial in the articulation of a new 'project'. Intellectuals were defined by their public status as well as their critical functions - of seeking to inform and 'critically intervene' in key events. Despite an early rapprochement with intellectuals around the Nexus network, the Demos and IPPR input, and the 'Giddens Roadshow', New Labour has become uneasy with the concept of intellectuals. Geoff Mulgan's to some extent justified critique of the 'academicisation of left intellectuals' seemed to be extended into a dismissal of the worth of intellectuals per se. For New Labour, intellectuals, like all other public sector professionals, need to 'get real', by coming up with practical policy proposals; the broader, critical, uncomfortable questioning, so crucial to intellectual life, is no longer necessary. Indeed it is noticeable that as Nexus continues to disintegrate, there is no outcry (as there would have been a decade ago) that this was confirmation of the dearth of left thinking. Rather, it seems that Nexus was a victim of its own success; that by contributing ideas-for-policy, and providing an intellectual gloss, it has exhausted its role. Bring on the Managers.

In contrast to the intellectual, it is the manager that drives New Labour's project. As usual New Labour has done its research; managers, according to Social Trends, are the second fastest rising social group (after 'personal and protective services'); while a recent poll in the *Guardian* found that 66 per cent of the population define themselves as 'managers' in one form or another. Managers are at the centre, rather than the margins, in touch with the 'populist mainstream', doers rather than thinkers, pragmatists rather than ideologues. Technically trained, they offer a new rationality, and conviction in the age of disenchantment, disillusion and fragmentation. With their empiricist and pseudo-scientific directives, they project themselves as the new experts, albeit dressed in grey suits rather than white coats. With their attacks on 'professional privilege', and language of 'outcomes' and 'targets', they are the spokespeople of the new meritocratic (rather than chattering) classes.

Agency versus structure

New Labour has been quick to embrace new individual aspirations; it has made itself the 'meritocratic party', through its unstinting belief that individuals, with the right education, training and work opportunities can make it. The belief in personal agency is however 'individualised' to an extent that removes any structural context. This distinguishes it sharply from the New Left's stress on agency, in which, freed from the trappings of 'economic determinism' and paternalistic statism, the capacities for 'empowerment', or greater autonomy, nevertheless rested upon the removal of socio-economic obstacles. They depended moreover on a critique of technocratic managerialism and the ends to which it was proceeding. If we take higher education as an example, it is worth remembering that the importance of transforming the value-system - the purpose as well as the nature of the institutions themselves - in order to move towards a more democratic culture was at the root of the New Left position, notably in the events around 1968. It is not surprising that adult education was also central in the work of many New Left intellectuals, for it contained not only a 'second chance', but redefined the concept of education by finding a new critical link between education values and wider societal values. In this respect, 'lifelong learning', a central component of New Left thinking, often stood in contrast to the narrow goals of the economic marketplace.

The trouble is that New Labour has moved from the - justifiable - critique of 'economic determinism', to a rejection of any structural causal factors. From a position which argued that economic or class position was not the only factor in shaping a child's educational opportunities (for example), it has proceeded to one which suggests that it is not a factor at all, certainly not when it is set against bad teaching. Perhaps the concept of 'structures', like 'systems', is a bit 'Grosvenor Squareish'. Structural explanations are also, of course, in need of a long-term perspective, carry costs and do not fall easily into populist language. Ironically, although at the micro level personal agency is everything, at the macro level there is an assumption that any capacity to shape events has been lost in the assimilation of politics into (neo-liberal) economics, leaving as a non-starter the prospect of major political change, or of offering a critical challenge to the global marketplace.

The importance of class

In his book *The Uses of Literacy*, a notable companion to Raymond Williams's *Culture and Society*, Richard Hoggart distinguishes between what he calls a 'good classlessness' and a 'bad classlessness'.[9] The negative aspects included what he described as a populist 'faceless' culture of consumerism, while the more positive aspects included the ways in which a common culture could be developed which broke down elitism, privilege and social hierarchies and replaced them with shared aspirations and open rather than closed cultural forms.

New Labour has its own good and bad classlessness. It has helped to modernise a range of state institutions, removing privilege from the House of Lords, and tradition from Westminster and the constitution; it has encouraged the recognition of generational shifts and initiated at least the prospect of the 'feminisation of politics' and the liberalisation of institutions. While these reforms reflect some of the concerns of the 'Nairn-Anderson' (New Left) critique of the antiquarian and deferential nature of Britain's ancien regime, they also clearly are conceptualised as being part of a shift towards a classless culture of opportunity and meritocratic achievement. The 'paradigm shift' from equality to inclusion is the key to this, and has helped to organise many of New Labour's policy agendas. Yet such a shift leaves issues of conflict, inequality and division untouched; it is as if these will be resolved of their own accord, or that social subjects can be 'focus-grouped into position'.[10] Nor does the distinction between a 'good rich' (Richard Branson) and a 'bad rich' (hereditary peers), on the basis of how the wealth was accumulated ('hard work' or 'privilege') provide an answer to major and deepening class inequalities.[11]

The New Left was also concerned about classlessness and, in its different moments, sought to engage with the changing contours of class politics, whether in the pursuit of a democratic culture, in its critique of the 'affluent society' thesis, in taking on the challenge of social movements, or its analysis of the emergence of post-fordist work systems. The New Left's commitment to class, contrary to general opinion, remained as central in the *Manifesto For New Times* as it did in earlier New Left perspectives. Crucially, this wasn't an unproblematic understanding of class; it drew on a range of perspectives which addressed the way in which class identity and class cultures were fragmenting, and the effects this had on communities, as well as the resulting changes in the relationship between class and politics. Stuart Hall, for example, writing over forty years

9. R. Hoggart, *The Uses of Literacy*, Penguin 1957, pp342-43.
10. S. Hall, *Marxism Today*, October-November 1998, p9.
11. See D. Goodhart for this distinction in *Prospect* August-September 1999.

ago on the emergence of mass consumption, noted the way in which transformations of class identity led to confusions over a perceived 'classlessness', and argued that capitalist restructuring brought with it different, if complex, forms of exploitation. [12] In the 1980s writers like Beatrix Campbell and Jeremy Seabrook looked at the way traditional class communities were breaking up, and at the forms of alienation and divisions that resulted; there was also, however, a recognition of the way in which communities were resisting and helping to negotiate the 'costs' of economic and social change. This was quite different from New Labour's attempts to remove the politics of class, in its own version of the classless utopia - the imagined community of middle England, the site of the new guilt-free aspirational existence, with its unlimited ladders of opportunity. It has been left to Roy Hattersley, the voice of Old Labour, to point out the obvious: 'you only need ladders in a hierarchical society' (*New Statesman*, January 99).

The re-birth of the SDP?

New Labour's own idea of modernisation therefore differs sharply from the New Left's attempts to rethink modernity. Though New Labour is reluctant to draw on history as a form of identification, there does exist an historical 'modernising' ancestry that explains much both about its development and its likely future faultlines. The parallel to be drawn is with the Social Democratic Party (SDP). All of the main political positions of the dissenters who defected from the Labour Party have been adopted by New Labour as the central planks of modernisation: reform of the Party's relationship with the trade unions; the adoption of a more pro-European position; the defeat of left activists; and the commitment to constitutional reform. Following the SDP, New Labour has declared the need to 'break the mould' of British politics, to 'go beyond left and right', to move away from conflict and class and 'adversarial politics'. More than this the SDP embraced the 'middle ground' (in Bill Rogers' words); it sought a meritocratic culture, which was reflected not only in its politics but in the social composition of the party itself - almost 60 per cent of its members were from the professional and managerial classes.

For the late Raphael Samuel, writing shortly after the SDP's formation in

---

12. S. Hall, 'A Sense of Classlessness', *Universities and Left Review* 5, autumn 1958.

1981, the latter's claim to modernity was projected through a relentless show of novelty and imagery; the SDP assumed itself - wrongly - to be the representatives of a new 'classlessness', offering an approach which was 'flexible' as opposed to 'rigid', 'clear-thinking' rather than 'dogmatic', and 'radical, but reasonable'.[13] In fact, he argued, what defined its political identity more than anything else was precisely its class location: it was the party of a 'newly unified middle class', which, in its hostility to ghettoised council estates, its rejection of the culture of organised labour, and its distaste for working class habits, was 'much too fastidious to touch a man who is beery': it sought to 'abolish the working class' (*Island Stories*, p261). This would be the confirmation that society could be reformed without specific claims to community; Samuel described their leading members as 'educational technocrats, fainthearted feminists, career politicians ... one time progressives and ideas men enjoying a second youth' ... originating characteristically ... 'from nowhere', they 'positively rejoice in the absence of regional or local ties'. This, he concluded, was indicative of a 'delighted act of self-recognition by a new class coming out and discovering its common identity' (pp270, 263).

New Labour has followed the SDP in taking class off the political agenda, as if the removal of complex social polarities can be turned into targets to be delivered by the appropriate line manager (but don't ask Prescott). Its broader understanding of modernity is itself shaped by a sense of almost pre-given certainties. For too long it has got away with the view that the major socio-economic transformations and political upheavals of the last three decades lead to only one version of globalisation, only one type of welfare agenda, only one value-system. In eschewing any historical reflection, or the need to engage with the more complex cultural transformations, it will remain both conservative and short-termist, leaving unaddressed the big question of how to 'reinvent modernity'[14] - which is the central issue for the New Left and its successors.

I am grateful to members of the Signs of the Times Group for ongoing discussions around many of the themes discussed in this article.

13. R. Samuel, *Island Stories*, Verso 1998, p263.
14. See Doreen Massey, editorial, *Soundings* 12, summer 1999.

Confronting breast cancer

Marve's story

A Photo Essay
by Cherron Lee Johnson

When I discovered that one of my closest friends, Marve Davis, aged 36, had breast cancer I decided to do something to highlight the issue for my final photographic project for my media degree at the University of Westminster. Marve was also eager to promote breast cancer awareness particularly for black women, as research shows that black women get the disease at a younger age, have more aggressive cancer cells, and are more likely to die unless the disease is found in the early stages. Marve worked with the charity, Cancer Black Care, who have highlighted these facts from research published in 1997 by Washington University, where work continues.

'It has been 5 months since I have been diagnosed with cancer. Every day when I wake, there are those first few moments when the memory of it doesn't exist, and then I remember, and the roller coaster of emotions engulfs my day until it is time to sleep again.'

This research recognises that black women need higher levels of radiotherapy and chemotherapy. Hence Marve has just completed her second treatment. However, her doctor now recognises that

if she had been given higher dosages initially, she possibly would not have had the need to continue her treatment.

Marve states: 'I have researched breast cancer in this country, and in comparison with the US. My conclusion is that the seriousness of breast cancer is not understood here by the authorities, particularly concerning the ethnic minorities.'

This project was not just about black women but to help stimulate all women into taking responsibility for their own health, and indeed men too. This is very poignant

'I am so tired and confused for searching for the reason why such a thing could have happened to me.'

because the lump was found in Marve's breast not by her but her partner.

Breast cancer is an ugly disease, and an issue that many women do not like to confront. Marve is obviously very attractive, and by working with her on this subject matter interesting dilemmas and contradictions could be addressed, especially about female identity today's media-led society.

So often the fashion industry promotes an ill and thin look that is sold to us as desirable and beautiful. What I wanted to explore was how people would respond to a beautiful women who is really very ill, but does not look as ill as the models portrayed in popular magazines. I wanted to force the viewer to acknowledge that breast cancer, like other diseases, does not discriminate. I wanted to challenge the image of an ill person looking ill and possibly close to death.

Marve first embarked upon this project because it would be a public way of exposing something that could affect us all directly or indirectly. Stimulating people to confront uncomfortable subjects, which could provoke self-reflection and examination and therefore greater prevention of death, was very important to us both.

The album we made offered Marve a personal record of this time, which she wanted to be able to look back on, but it also provided an extension of my original theme of exploring a personal space. It challenged the voyeuristic curiosity in all of us when dealing with a taboo issue. The original book cover was purposely made fragile, allowing the viewer to be aware they were entering a personal space to be handled with care and sensitivity.

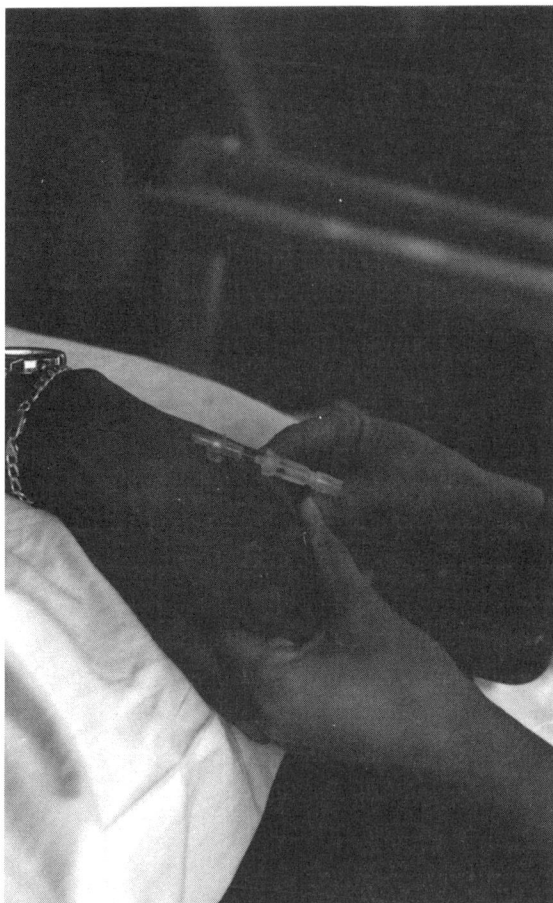

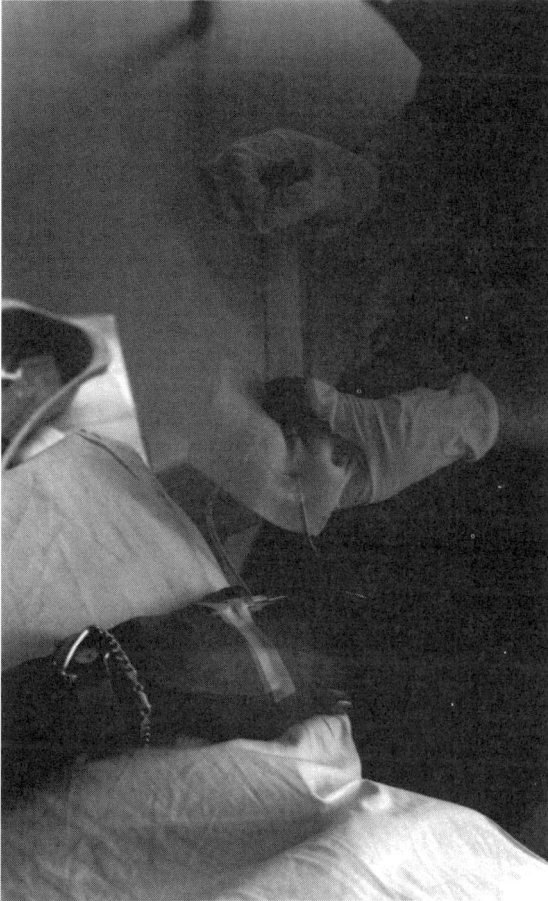

By first entering Marve's space the viewer is taken on an intimate path again; then this abruptly changes through images of Marve having her routine chemotherapy. As the photographer I was struck by the fact that the act of receiving chemotherapy, which for me is so intensely personal, takes place in the day

room, a very public space, demonstrating how issues of the 'public' and 'private' converge.

As a survivor, and not a victim, it was important for the final image to convey Marve's inner strength and courage, with the rays of sunlight beaming on her face as she tends to flowers in the comfort of her home

Storming the Millennium
The New Politics of Change
Edited by Tim Jordan and Adam Lent

Recommended retail price £12.99. Available to *Soundings* readers for £10.99 post free.

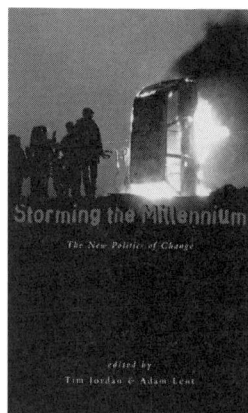

As the new millennium begins, activists are reflecting on their struggles, and journalists and intellectuals are recognising the importance of the new politics of change. *Storming the Millennium* is the first book to bring a range of activists and intellectuals together and it provides some of the first histories of movements at the core of new politics, grappling with the important political and theoretical issues they raise.

Bringing together new and established writers, *Storming the Millennium* includes discussions of crime and justice, disabilities, bisexual, gay, lesbian and transgender politics, race issues in 1990s Britain and activism on the Internet. It also addresses the relationship between new politics, the new left and socialism.

Contributors: Peter Beresford, Tessa Bird, Patrick Field, Tony Fitzpatrick, Nancy Fraser, Stuart Hall, Shirin Housee, Rupa Huq, Tim Jordan, Adam Lent, Doreen Massey, Michael Rustin, Sanjay Sharma, Merl Storr.

Please send cheque for £10.99 made out to Lawrence and Wishart to L&W, 99a Wallis Road London E9 5LN.

Five poems

Seizure

I fell down on the grass
My heart bumped and jolted
Each heart beat collapsed on me
Like a wall and crushed me.
Then the bulb smashed
I lay on the topsoil.
I lay on the subsoil.
I went down to the earth's mantle.
I slurred and twisted
Among hot glands of rock,

& saw, way up,
on the flighty rim of the earth
A man in a coat like mine
A man with a life like mine
Who ran and danced a few paces
Then fell down on the grass.

Geoffrey Adkins

Aground

To say 'we struck a sandbank', makes it sound
hard, or sudden, when all we felt was an easing
up against something, and then a ceasing,
unbalancing like bracing for an imagined wind.

But by the ship's master's furious cry:
'Shalla!', shouted orders, the rush of bare feet
slapping iron gangways, by the rising note
of the engine – by these things we knew.

All night, our lights have carved the same thin row
of date palms, on the same stretch of broken bank,
from the black universe, and the crew's best

effort can only slew us round the bow
like rooted water-weed. By the rails, a man
turns, mid-prayer, toward his new West.

Susanne Ehrhardt

Easter 1999

The camelia beyond my mother's kitchen door:
a breast full of medals, all over scarlet, in the rain.

My dear one in Sarajevo tomorrow
will drive to Zagreb along hairpin roads,

the Sarajevan airport closed ten days now.
Of the misery and exodus further south she can hardly speak,

she hisses over the static - or is it the static:
I hate all politicians -

I'll never vote again -
Nobody here agrees with -

In Belgrade a tyrant arms himself with
sheaves of gladioli on a table polished as boots.

Kosovo blossoms

Heart of mine, take care, drive slow.

Judith Kazantzis

Milk

Mother and child are keeping
a naked new decorum
as if sleep's trowel was gardening
a wild of bedclothes off them

her breasts, his head, together
one side warmed by his breathing,
first scene of son with mother
him filled, enthralled, her fading

like deer come from the forest;
two exiles of this garden;
one, tame to him, came nearest
and fed him milk of Eden.

Robin Leanse

Field of Vision

What happens to shadows when the light
absents itself? Is there a gathering up
of the indistinct, like pastry scraps
to make one sharp-edged leaf or lattice?

And the volume in this enamel bowl:
was it always present, if only now
made visible, defined by the meniscus
of emptiness brimming lip to lip?

Why ask? ... once having seen
a patch of yellow - yellow grass
stencilled where a tent was staked
and then the whole field entirely

free from contingency: no haze
of unsown flax, no subtle after-
image contradicting the retina;
nothing less than this sufficiency

- dazzling plain, green, utterly.

Gregory Warren Wilson

Letter from Turkey

Fred Halliday

Fred Halliday visited Turkey earlier in the year and wrote a piece for Soundings *looking at contemporary challenges to the Ataturk legacy. He has added a second article commenting on the effects of the earthquakes which devastated Turkey in August.*

There is no better way to grasp the conflicts of interest and identity definition that rend this fascinating country than to observe the fate of its most outstanding shrines. Ankara, the Anatolian town which has served as the capital since Ataturk moved it from Istanbul in 1923, was until recently dominated by one building: the Anitkabir, the tomb of Ataturk himself, a neoclassical columned structure shorn of all religious or Middle Eastern associations. The visitor approaches through an entrance flanked by heroic statues, symbolising liberation and the emancipation of women, and along a solemn avenue. It is here that all official foreign visitors pay their respects: on the day I visited it, there was a wreath from the Democratic Turkish League of Kosovo. On the steps up to the main hall are the words *Hakimiyet Milletindir*, 'Sovereignty to the People' - at once an appropriation of the message of the French revolution and a rejection of the claims of Sultan and religious authority alike.

This is the shrine of the Ataturkist legacy, one based on an individual, that remains, to a degree almost unknown anywhere else in the modern world, the ideology of the state: Ataturk's picture, bust, lapel buttons, postcards are seen throughout the country. Museums display his clothes, his cigarette cases, the text of his famous six-day speech, the *buyuk nutuk*, and, in more questionable vein, photographs of cloud formations and shadows that appear to represent his profile, or eyes. He is the *murshit* (the guide), the *ebedi cef* (the immortal leader), the *halackar gazi* (the saviour warrior). The state promotes this reverence, as do those, notably educated women, who fear the Islamist advance. Many respect him for his decisiveness, in breaking with both the religious and imperial pasts. 'If he was alive we would have built a metro in Istanbul long ago', one intellectual remarked to me. 'Why can't they grow up and take decisions themselves', remarked another. All is not, however, as it appears: there are also those opposed to Ataturk's legacy who mask their subversion in an exaggerated cult.

The challenge to this legacy has been long in the brewing, and is from several directions. One now exists as an alternative focus in Ankara itself: the Islamist municipal authorities have erected the Kocatepe Mosque, which rises in the city centre, floodlit at night in challenge to the shrine. (The Kocatepe is, to western eyes, an incongruous symbol: beneath it is a parking lot and a shopping mall.) This is not the end of Islamist aspirations: in Istanbul they hope to build a comparable mosque at the city centre, Taksim Square; and some militants have demonstrated regularly in favour of the reconversion of Aya Sophia, long a museum, into a place of Muslim worship. For many Turks this rise in the public demonstration of Islamist power, as in the Kocatepe, is an insult: in 1997 hundreds of thousands of people marched through Ankara protesting against *irtica*, reaction, in rejection of the claims of the Islamists to redefine Turkish society. They protested at what the Islamists had done in power, be it as mayors of Istanbul and Ankara, or in their period in office, in coalition with the Dogru Yol (True Path) party of Tansu Ciller.

A very different clash of symbols and programmes can be observed at the holiest shrine of Istanbul, the Eyup Mosque, named after Ayyoub al-Ansari, one of the associates of the Prophet Mohammad, who died during the siege of what was then Constantinople in 674-8. The mosque is a symbol of both the Islamic and the Ottoman pasts. And if the main appeal of the Islamists is to a religious heritage, to a just society or *adil duzen*, and defence of Turkish *akhlak* (morals) against foreign influences, and tourists, one of their other resorts has been to appropriate the Ottoman past. The Ataturkists also appropriate some of the Ottoman past, but dislike the dilution of Turkish identity associated with such institutions as the janissaries, recruits from the Christian regions of Europe, and later, decadent, and opportunistically pan-Islamist, rulers such as Sultan Abdul Hamid (1876-1909).

A beautiful collection of shrines on the upper reaches of the Golden Horne, the Eyup was immortalised for western literature in the writings of the French novelist Pierre Loti. It was to the Eyup that the Ottoman Sultans came to be crowned as *padishah*, or king of kings. Its Islamic and Ottoman pasts can be seen in the alms that are still distributed to the needy, or in the couples who come to have their marriages blessed, or to seek a cure for their problems. The neighbourhood is dominated by Islamists, as is that of neighbouring Fatih, site of the mosque built by Sultan Mehmet, the conqueror of the city in 1453 who rode his horse into Aya Sofya and had it kick over the vessels on the altar. Bearded men and covered women dominate the streets. But this Islamist atmosphere mingles with the revival, and instrumentalisation, of the Ottoman past: thus a cafe just outside the Eyup is called the *Hunkar*, the word for the Sultan's throne. On the Friday morning before Bayram, the feast of the sacrifice, as sheep and calves were being brought in for symbolic slaughter, the streets were enlivened by a *mehter* band, a group of musicians dressed in Ottoman military uniforms, and chain mail, playing martial music to the rhythm of two steps forward, one backward. (Some take the *mehter* step to be symbolic of modern Turkey as a whole.) In their attempt to promote this appropriation of the Ottoman past, Islamist publishing houses produce books on the great victories of the Ottoman military commanders, and idealise the Tulip Age, the first three decades of the eighteenth century.

The contrast with Iran is striking. In Iran empire and monarch were associated with the modernising, secular, state, hence Islamism is republican; in Turkey the state, under Ataturk, sought to reject the Ottoman past - its institutions, its empire, its clothes, its script - and hence Islamism is monarchical. Turkey is one European country where you will not find any complexes about the imperial past. As with other European imperial states, the empire has, very much, come home: waves of immigrants from the Balkans, the Caucasus and Central Asia have settled here, and they are now joined by communities of the 'suitcase trade', from the former Soviet republics. In a symbolic gesture, the body of Enver Pasha, a Young Turk leader who died fighting the Bolsheviks in Central Asia, has been brought back to Istanbul and buried with his associates in Independence Park.

Since 1984 another challenge to the Ataturkist legacy has been the war in the southern-eastern part of the country, between the Turkish army and the guerrillas of the PKK, the Workers' Party of Kurdistan. Many thousands have died, over three thousand villages have been destroyed, and hundreds of thousands have been made refugees. The war is estimated to have cost $7 billion a year, roughly equal to the net cost to London of its role in Northern Ireland. The PKK itself is a descendant of the militarised far left of the 1960s and 1970s. When it began its armed struggle in 1984 it is doubtful if it had widespread support: but the response of the Turkish state, and the lack of a legitimate space of Kurdish political demands, have led to the growth of PKK support far beyond its initial base. This broader Kurdish support has, combined with the impasse of the guerrilla resistance itself, had a moderating influence, in that the PKK no longer demands independence.

The Turkish state itself has, however, given little ground: the state refuses to recognise as minorities any communities other than those stipulated in the 1923 Treaty of Lausanne. The constitution includes a clause, itself denoted as unchangeable, on the indivisibility of Turkey and on the monopoly of the Turkish language - this precludes not just secession, but what most would regard as any meaningful regional autonomy. Several parties seen as representing a Kurdish interest have been harassed and suppressed: state policy has, in this way, promoted the hegemony of the PKK over Kurdish intellectual and political life. There has been some movement in the 1990s: Kurdish is now permitted in public places, and the derogatory phrase for Kurds, *dag turkler*, 'mountain Turks', is no longer used. Both President Demirel and his predecessor President Ozal have recognised the existence of a Kurdish community, and the press reports openly on the issue - though not on the progress of the war. One newspaper columnist wrote an article under the title 'Atakurd' - a play on Ata, meaning father of - and speculating on how Turks would feel if things had turned out the other way. And there are many in public life, including the Turkish employers' federation TUSIAD, who have called for a political solution. A report by the Migration Commission of the parliament blamed the security forces, and in particular the 'Special Teams' who are held responsible for particular persecution of the Kurds, for mass emigration from the south-east. The report called, for the first time in Turkey's history, for official recognition of a Kurdish identity.

The problem goes back, however, to the military: they are still, in most if not all significant respects, the effective rulers of Turkey. On the Kurdish question, as on other issues, such as Cyprus, they hold the key. While the range of public discussion and awareness of the Kurdish issue has expanded very substantially in recent years, few people I spoke to saw any prospect of a significant move on the Kurdish issue in the years ahead. But if Turkish nationalism in its more extreme form has adopted some questionable claims, predictably, repression from above is matched by some alternative simplification from below: the *Turkish Daily News* of 3 April 1998 printed an interview with the head of a Kurdish cultural foundation who argued that, since the Turks had no word of their own for 'thank you', using either a French (*mersi*) or Arabic (*tesekkur*) word, they were 'a rude people who were unable to express appreciation'.

'The derogatory phrase for Kurds, *dag turkler*, 'mountain Turks', is no longer used'

The Ataturkist legacy has also come under attack from another, modernising, current, known, at least by its enemies, as the 'second republicans'. They accept much of what Ataturk did but argue that the time has come to move on: to fulfil that integration of Turkey into Europe which the *gazi* began; to liberalise - towards the left, and towards Kurds, as much as towards women who wish to wear the headscarf; to end the brutality that still marks the activities of the Turkish police; and above all to get the military out of politics. Much of Turkish life is overshadowed by the security organisations - the army, and MIT, the political police - in a way that civilian politicians do not control, and with underhand links to the mafia. Turkey's most prominent writer, Yasar Kemal, himself a Kurd, argues that the number one problem facing the country is human rights. Some have also argued for a more open, critical, account of the massacre of Armenians in World War I. This critique of the authoritarian, outmoded, conception of Turkish identity and interests is articulated by human rights groups: the disruption by the Istanbul police chief of a meeting between the European Union representative in Turkey and a group of NGOs he had invited to his office is cited as typical of the archaic attitudes of the security forces. In their own rendering of the Ottoman legacy, some secular left intellectuals contrast its diversity, and cultural cosmopolitanism, with the centralism that has pervaded Turkish reformers from the mid-nineteenth century onwards. Not for nothing was the military regime that came to power in 1908 called the Committee of Union and Progress.

No-one should have any doubt as to the fact that the military are in charge, and the military would not want it any other way: television news on the night of 27 March 1998 led with film of the monthly meeting of the National Security Council, where civilian politicians meet - i.e. are given their instructions by - the top military personnel. The body language of assertion on one side, and embarrassed attentiveness on the other, told it all: the politicians were instructed to clamp down further on the Islamists or face the consequences, which would be another military coup. For Ataturkists, on the other hand, the 'second republicans' are a group of dreamers, a product of an Istanbul elite that has never reconciled itself to the power of Ankara. The miserable showing (under 1 per cent) of one party that embodied its programme, that of Cem Boyner, in the elections of 1995 is taken as showing how little real following they have. More seriously, the Ataturkists charge that the 'second republicans' are a fifth column, promising disintegration of the country, the unchallenged advance of the Islamists, and a descent into chaos. Like others in the region the Ataturkist elite has drawn its own lessons from the collapse of the USSR: they do not intend to make the same mistake.

Much hinges, inevitably, on an assessment of the Islamist forces themselves, and of the challenge they pose. Some parties are openly secularist, and support the ban on headscarves. The litany of Islamist provocations is many: their leader Erkakan, a man with a long record of support for nationalist causes (he advocated the occupation of the whole of Cyprus in 1974), and, a rare thing in Turkey, an exponent of anti-Semitic views, has said that they will come to power by the ballot or by force. Some mayors have refused to shake hands with women, some have sought to enforce a ban on male doctors treating women, some have forced women employees to choose between wearing the scarf and standing in the street all day counting cars. The leaders have been careful to keep within the law: Fethullah Gulen, the leader of one group, that claims to be inspired by the model of Pakistan, has argued that 95 per cent of Islam's programme is not political. But this has not done them much good: Erbakan has just been banned from political life for five years, and his Refah party, a coalition that he successfully held together, had to change its name to

Fazlile (Virtue) party, while his successors fell to squabbling over his inheritance. A strong candidate to succeed him was the mayor of Istanbul, Recep Tayyip Erdogan: but he ran into difficulties after he declared in 1997 that 'the minarets are bayonets, the domes helmets, the mosques our barracks, the believers our soldiers'. He gave every sign of meaning business and was prosecuted as a result. Fethullah's apparent moderation, on the other hand, has won him few friends: there are open allegations that his project of a 'safe' Islamism is inspired by foreign powers - America, or, failing them, Germany. One secularist intellectual who visited the television station controlled by Fethullah was struck by what he found: a building peopled only by men. Fethullah is, he insisted, surrounded by a lot of dangerous looking bearded young men. My own encounter with the correspondent of Fethullah's paper *Zaman* was not reassuring: he asked me for my views of Pakistan, and when I told him about the political chaos, ethnic conflict, and narcotics trading, he put down his pencil. The interview had ended.

It is, for outsiders as much as for Turks, hard to get a handle on the Islamist current in this formally secular country. In the elections of 1995 they won, in the form of the Refah, 21 per cent of the votes in national elections, and control of many cities. Parallel to the growth of Islamist parties, there has been a revival of unofficial Muslim organisations, notably the *tarikats* or sects, banned by Ataturk - a sort of pluralised freemasonry, which now pervades business and political life. There is also a thriving Islamist business sector: posters on the road in from Istanbul airport advertise the Ihlas Finance Group, and the Albaraka Bank (*ihlas* is an Islamic term for devotion, *baraka* for blessing); travel companies sport names like Hilal (Crescent); there are Islamist fashion houses, and perfume shops in the name of Furkan – which means, literally 'The Divider' i.e. between truth and falsity, and is a name for the Koran. The signs of a growing public pietism are evident in cafes, where the food, music and even chairs have been changed to conform to a more traditional model. All of this has, however, its limits: alcohol is freely available, the press has a wide range of comment and bodily display, there is none of the public prostration at prayer time that is commonplace in Egypt or Saudi Arabia.

There are, however, other problems with any evaluation of this Islamist challenge. The first difficulty is with the official conception of secularism. This, one of Ataturk's six 'revolutionary principles', is taken, off the shelf of enlightenment values as it were, from the French revolution: hence the Turkish work *laiklik*. What it means in reality is not atheism, or the exclusion of religion from public life, but state control, and appropriation of, religion. Through the National Religious Directorate the state pays the salaries, and thereby controls the Friday speeches, of 180,000 clergy. It is now attempting not to close, but to bring under state control, another 10,000 or so unauthorised mosques. For all its repudiation of the Arabic and Muslim past, the very language of Ataturkism is replete with Islamic symbolism: thus the Turkish flag displays the Islamic crescent, the word used for Ataturk on every school playground bust is *murshit*, the 'guide', a term of Islamic resonance. The national liberation struggle that defeated the Greeks, French and British in the early 1920s is the *milli mucadele*, both *milli* and *mucadele* being words with religious connotations. Secularism is conceived of not, as in most other countries, as a matter of degree, and as a cognate of tolerance, but as opposition to all that the secular and authoritarian elite despise. Small wonder then that the opposition to this Ataturkist experiment has been growing over the decades: the roots lie in the opposition of small towns, traditional elites, to the state in the 1940s. Twice, in 1960 and 1971 the military intervened to arrest the process. But in 1980, faced with a militant left, the military to some degree endorsed Islamism: like the Israelis with Hamas, and the FLN with the FIS, the response was to promote Islamism, hopefully controlled, to diminish the left.

For their part the Islamists offer a mishmash of ideas, articulated with a mixture of quotes from the Koran and the Prophet, and ideas taken from late twentieth century discourse of opposition. In book fairs and book shops the Islamists offer a wide range of texts - studies on the holy texts, replete with such studies as of 'hypocrites in Islam', and of the devil, teach yourself manuals, accounts of the Ottoman period, studies of western corruption via globalisation and the media, and translations from a selection of western literature: predictable entries such as Tolstoy's *Hajji Murat*, and Walter Scott's *Saladin* together with works deemed to have an appropriate, and appropriable, moral message, including *Crime and Punishment*, *Don Quixote*, *Faust* and *Coriolanus*. Those themes in contemporary western thinking that suit the challenge to the Turkish state are also happily recruited: much is made of the Ottoman practice of multiculturalism, now linked to the recently imported idea of *farklikik*, 'difference', while a best-seller in Islamist bookshops has been Paul

Feyerabend's *Against Method*. Concepts have a way of being turned to strange uses in the Turkish concept: thus the term enlightenment has been appropriated by the far left, in its Turkish form - *aydinlik* - while in its Islamic form *tenvir* - it has become a watchword of the Islamists. This leaves the original concept with the, enlightened but authoritarian, state. The question that secularists in Turkey repeatedly pose is both clear, and unanswerable: 'Will the Turkish Islamists take Turkey down the road of Iran, Algeria, Afghanistan?' The arguments against are obvious enough: so far, the Islamists have not resorted to mass violence; Turkey is a very different kind of society; the leaders of the main Islamist faction have made some reasonable, conciliatory, noises. None of this cuts much ice with secularists. First of all, it was thought that such countries as Iran, or Lebanon, or for that matter Algeria, were immune to such mass authoritarian religious movements: but they were not. Secondly, the issue of violence is not so clear: there has been no resort to urban guerrilla warfare in Turkey, that place being reserved for the very unreligious, militantly Marxist-Leninist PKK; but secularist writers have been the target of murder - among them Turan Dursin, Cetin Emec and Ugur Mumcu, all accused of criticising Islamists and, most spectacularly, the 37 participants at a conference in Sivas in 1993, organised by the late Aziz Nesim, defender of Salman Rushdie; some were burnt to death by an Islamist mob and the survivors were beaten by the local, Islamist-controlled, fire brigade who were called to rescue them. As one generally critical Turkish intellectual put it to me: 'These people have not engaged in mass killings, not yet'.

Perhaps the most vulnerable group of all in Turkey are those from the Islamic minority sect, the Alevis, comprising up to 20 per cent of the total Turkish population: as virtually everywhere else in the Muslim world, such minorities, faced with a potentially dominant Islamist majority, are themselves secularist (as are the Baluch and Pathans in Pakistan, the Kurds in Iran, the Kabyles in Algeria). Some of the worst Islamist violence, mediated through the hands of the Istanbul police, has been against Alevis, regarded by Islamists as not proper Muslims. Much use is also made of the word *takiye*: in Islam, particularly Shi'ite Islam, this means dissimulation, in face of tyrannical government, in other words concealment of political goals. Erbakan, Fethullah and the others are therefore charged with *takiye*, and not to be trusted.

The largest problem does not lie, however, in the realm of intention. For what is evident from reading, and listening to, the Turkish Islamists, as with their confreres in other countries, is that they may not be dissimulating, but rather may well believe everything they say: one prominent spokesman, the brother of the late President Ozal, assured an endless late night TV discussion I had the dubious satisfaction of participating in, that since Islam was a religion of love, everything would be solved when a government true to its ideals came to power. The Islamists get a large Kurdish vote - more than the semi-legal Kurdish parties: but this may be more a form of protest than of identification with the Islamist programme. When asked about the Kurdish issue the standard reply is that since all Turks are Muslims there is no problem. What their record in office, at local and national level, has shown is that while on particular symbolic issues, such as veiling, they have a view, of a retrograde kind, on the broader challenges facing the country they do not have coherent policies. Their economic policy is the very secular, early modernist, one of industrialisation in small towns. It all turns out to be a confused and mediocre mess, much indulged by kindly western searchers for authenticity, and attractive to a mass of recently arrived rural migrants, but of scant relevance to the problems of Turkey today. In such a context, of intellectual vacuity and national crisis, the Islamists could easily lapse into violence, whatever benign words their spokesmen currently offer.

These debates on Turkish politics and identity are inevitably exacerbated by changes in the global environment. Turkey belongs to three worlds - to Europe, which has since Ataturk been the official point of reference, to the Middle East, with which, despite Ataturk, Turkey has developed commercial and political ties since the 1970s, and to the newly emergent *dunya*, the world of Turkic states and communities, stretching, in the words of president Demirel, 'from the Pamirs to the Adriatic': this compromises the Uighur in Chinese Sinjiang, the Central Asian states (Turkmenistan, Uzbekistan, Kirghizya, Kazakhstan), the northern, mainly Uzbek region of Afghanistan, Azerbaijan in the Transcaucasus, the numerous peoples of the northern Caucasus, and, in the Balkans, Bosnia, Albania and Kosovo.

Whether Turkey is or is not part of Europe is, as it is with Russia, an empty argument: it has been so for five hundred years. But the attempt to become part of the European Union has foundered, and is unlikely to succeed in the foreseeable future: while Turkey enjoys trading access, fears of migration, human rights violations, the domination of the military, and the financial burden Turkish membership would impose, all add up to an enduring holding operation on political union. After the Luxembourg summit of December 1997, where Turkey was excluded from the list of next applicants, premier Mesut Yilmaz broke off contacts with the EU. Many in Turkey oppose this, seeing in the European link an important bastion against Islamist advance: the military criticised Yilmaz for his critical stance on Europe.

The Middle Eastern connection has been a mixed blessing: trade has declined since the Iraqi invasion of Kuwait in 1980, and there are fears of fundamentalist influence from the Arab states, especially Libya and Saudi Arabia. In the last three years Turkey has consolidated its military relationship with Israel: this makes sense in Ankara, given the fear of Syrian-backed Kurdish guerrilla operations, but has led to a growing antagonism in relations with the Arab world. The Turks themselves do not seem too worried: they put the blame on the Arabs. They also seem to get on well with Israelis, 'it is one country where we are treated as equals' said an academic observer.

As for the *dunya*, it is has turned out to be a mixed blessing: Turkish small businesses and building contractors are active in Central Asia, and there is enormous interest, for reasons of economic security and of prestige, in the construction of oil and gas pipelines from the Caspian region through Turkey. But six inefficient, very corrupt and authoritarian former Soviet republics, with bad communications and infrastructure, are not a global option. Most of Turkish trade is with Europe, most of its investment goes into Russia and the Ukraine, rather than the *dunya*. The politics, and funding, of pipelines is itself very complex and there is, as yet, little certainty about how this energy will be shipped to the outside world.

Inevitably, the internal debate on identity, and the external debate on orientation, become intertwined. For the secularists the argument is clear: Turkey must be incorporated into Europe not so much because it is already ready to be but because this is the only way to consolidate democracy and human rights inside the country. For Turkic nationalists it was Ataturk's abandonment of the *dunya* that led to the country's isolation: they want to see a more militant line on Chechnya, Bosnia, Sinjiang, and Azerbaijan, as well as Cyprus. One of the more unusual additions to the public monuments of Istanbul is a shrine, just off the Hippodrome, to the 'martyrs of East Turkestan' i.e. the Chinese north-west.

In April 1998 the manageress of a Chinese restaurant in Istanbul was assassinated by East Turkestani militants. For the Islamists the option is the Middle East: they are not sure which one, of course, and Erbakan's experiences as premier, when he went to Libya professing Muslim solidarity and got a public scolding from Qaddafi on Turkish chauvinism, have not reinforced this aspiration. Erbakan is, however, undeterred: after his party was closed, he embarked on his 27th *hajj* or pilgrimage to Mecca.

Iran remains an uneasy neighbour: despite talk of historic enmity the two countries have lived on good terms for most of nearly six centuries. In the Topkapi palace there are gifts exchanged with Nadir Shah of Iran in the 1740s, in the Ataturk Mausoleum Museum, similar exchanges with Reza Shah in the 1930s. But there is also distrust. An Ottoman saying goes 'if you learn Persian, you lose half of your faith', a reference to the hedonistic influence of Hafez, Sa'adi and Omar Khayyam. Since 1979 Turkish secularists have feared the influence of the Iranian revolution: this has been confirmed by the refusal of Iranian officials to lay wreaths at Ataturk's tomb, preferring instead to visit the town of the Sufi saint Jalal al-Din Rumi, at Konya. Turkish envoys to Tehran have declined to visit the tomb of Imam Khomeini. The Iranian ambassador was expelled after taking part in a 'Jerusalem Day' organised by a Refah mayor near Ankara, where the Iranian envoy made an anti-secularist speech.

None of these issues allows of an easy, or rapid, solution. The military elite, and their civilian allies, who run Turkey continue to maintain an unbending, brittle, resistance to anything that smacks of weakness: authoritarian stubbornness at the top is matched by police and army brutality towards political dissent at the bottom. Yet much is changing. The press and 26 television channels are in large measure free and there is a vibrant intellectual, and cultural, life. Non-governmental organisations operate in a way unimaginable in Iran or the Arab world. It is possible to debate in public many issues that, even a decade ago, were taboo. This is a country with immense human, as well as natural, resources: its elite reflects a degree of astounding social mobility, something inherited from the Ottoman times. Its top universities produce graduates of world quality: the questioning after a series of seminars I gave in Istanbul and Ankara was at a higher level, and less given to irrelevant point-scoring, than in any other country I have visited.

At the same time the challenges faced by the semi-democratic institutions of Turkey are not imagined: in addition to the authoritarian immobilism of the military elite, there is hyperinflation in the economy, a retrograde, devious, and fecklessly vacuous Islamism at the mass level, a Kurdish opposition that replicates the worst of the authoritarian Marxist past, but which has now, in the face of state intransigence, come to hegemonise Kurdish politics in the country. The programme which Ataturk drew up in the 1920s was in many ways relevant then and remains so to this day: whether it can be altered, and developed, to meet the challenges of the contemporary world, and to conform to a definition of European modernity that has itself altered much in the ensuing seven decades, is a question that will for many years to come preoccupy the versatile people of Turkey. It will equally be of no little relevance to all three of the international communities - Europe, the Middle East, the *dunya* - to which Turkey belongs. *Spring 1999*

Turkey, Autumn 1999: Politics after the earthquakes

The earthquake that shook western Turkey on 17 August has had effects not only in the loss of tens of thousands of lives, and the destruction of large tracts of urban areas, estimated at $25 billion, but also on the political landscape of Turkey itself. Great natural disasters all have, as the world increasingly understands, a social and human dimension as well as a natural one: famines are in large part man-made, the impact of tornadoes, volcanoes, earthquakes is contained, or amplified by the character of the society in which it occurs

There is inevitably recrimination about whether such disasters could have been prevented, or foreseen. It is not only in developing societies that earthquakes occasion criticism of the state: there was much anger in Japan at government inactivity after the Kobe quake of 1995. In Nicaragua, the government's theft of emergency relief money after the quake of 1972 was a major contributing factor in the popular revolution that triumphed in 1979. Nature and humanity are both shaken by earthquakes: that of 17 August was no exception.

Immediately after the Turkish earthquake hit there were accusations that buildings had been built by greedy and incompetent speculators. The blame fell equally on the builders themselves and on the state building inspectors who were charged with complicity with the speculators. One owner of a construction firm, later arrested, openly admitted he had no qualifications and used sand

and seashells from the beaches to build his houses. But recrimination also follows earthquakes, and in two waves. The immediate, short-term, anger concerns the failure of the state to provide assistance to those buried under the rubble: for the first time in modern Turkey there was widespread anger at the failure of the army to assist. All the more so because the centre of the quake was at Golcuk, site of a major naval base: the military were quick to rescue their own buried colleagues; when local people telephoned

'"Istanbul was smitten because it is full of transvestites" one Islamist said'

for help they were told it was after five o'clock and they should call back the next day. The risks of a longer-run popular anger, if houses are not rebuilt and money is stolen - the scenario of Nicaragua - remains.

Anger at the inaction of the state was, however, as much a reflection of broader changes in Turkish society as a result of the inaction after 17 August. No state, however well prepared, could have responded to all the emergency needs of the stricken areas. The Turkish state does seem to have coped sufficiently with some of the major consequences of the disaster - providing emergency shelter, and preventing the outbreak of dangerous diseases. What lay behind some of the anger was a growing sense evident in recent years that the state, or elements in it, were involved in corrupt mafia-like activities.

But it was not only the state that was criticised. Some commentators pointed out that it was not sufficient to blame corrupt builders and speculators: those who bought houses they knew were not adequately constructed and who fuelled the construction boom were also criticised. So too were some of the religious and nationalist politicians who sought to benefit from the earthquake crisis: elements in the Virtue Party said that the quake was a punishment from God to the corrupt, decadent, world of Istanbul. 'Istanbul was smitten because it is full of transvestites', one Islamist said. The Islamists also pointed out that it was in the Golcuk base that the military had, in February 1998, taken the decision to ban its predecessor, the Rifah Party. In the aftermath of the earthquake, it was, however, not the Islamists who provided emergency social services - as they had done during the Cairo quake of 1992. It was, rather the selfsame decadent youth who rushed to help - young men with earrings, who joined with many other local, secular, people, to set up emergency civil organisations.

The earthquake cast a new light not only on Turkey's Islamists, however, but also on relations with two other, crucial, elements of the Turkish political landscape. One was relations with Greece: in an extraordinary outburst of solidarity, the mayor of Athens and other Greek officials went to Istanbul and provided emergency relief. A Turkish newspaper printed on its front page a 'Thank You' headline, *Evkharisto*, in Greek - something inconceivable before. Those who criticised the Greeks, and who implied that one of the leaders of the Turkish civilian relief effort was suspect because he was Jewish, were howled down. The sudden improvement in relations with Greece may, or may not, last. It was given tragic further impetus when a few weeks later Athens was hit by a smaller quake and a Turkish team came to help. But those in Greece, notably the Foreign Minister, Papandreou, who wish to improve relations with Turkey have taken rapid advantage of the earthquake to press for a change of policy: Athens has already announced that it is ending its veto on European Union aid to Turkey and is also willing to discuss eventual Turkish entry to the Union, provided this is on the same conditions as other applicants.

E qually dramatic, and of uncertain long-term significance, is the impact of the earthquake on the relations between the Turkish state and the Kurds. Already this year there has been a significant, and unexpected, shift in official policy as, in the aftermath of the trial of the guerrilla leader Abdullah Ocalan, the guerrillas have proclaimed that they will end their war. Ocalan may well be executed at some point in the future, but he has taken advantage of his current situation to launch an important political initiative. Some officials in Ankara have responded by urging a dialogue with Kurdish parties, and a recognition of the cultural rights of Kurds. The earthquake itself showed no distinction between Turk and Kurd: many Kurdish migrants live in the areas hit, and large amounts of assistance poured into Istanbul from the Kurdish region. All may collapse, but a possibility of further dialogue exists.

In many cultures, earthquakes occasion not only political and social consequences, but also broader reflections on life. In Turkey, as in all other countries, reaction is divided, into those who see such events as tragic, or as punishment for evil doing, and those who see it as an opportunity. Some commentators on the Turkish popular response suggested Turks would react fatalistically, invoking fate or kismet. But the Islamic tradition offers another view of such events: Sura 99 of the Koran, entitled zilzal or the earthquake, sees such convulsions as the moment at which a new era opens. Indeed revolutions are often compared to earthquakes precisely because, as processes that are out of human control, they undermine the old social order. In European culture, the most famous of all such events, the Lisbon earthquake of 1755, was taken by Voltaire as evidence of the imperfection of the world and the need for human initiative - prompting his satirical novel *Candide*. In more modern times, earthquakes are also taken as the metaphor for major political events: the most famous account of the Russian revolution of 1917, by the American writer John Reed was entitled *Ten Days that Shook the World*. It remains to be seen what the longer-run consequences for Turkey will be - if the quake signals an onset of crisis, debt and recrimination, or a political change among Turks, and in relations with the Kurds and Greece. It would ironic indeed if a natural event of this tragic dimension, were to have such dramatic, but positive, political and social consequences.

Rethinking 'global' city centres

The example of Birmingham

Nick Henry and Adrian Passmore

In the face of 'globalisation', boosterist strategies of regeneration have haunted cities for nearly two decades. Such strategies are often socially divisive, exclusive and homogenising; we argue for the possibilities of other 'global' paths of social and cultural investment in city building.

'Birmingham cancels Christmas'

So screamed the national headlines of November 1998 as Birmingham City Council announced the Winterval'98 promotion of the city's lights, entertainments, events and exhibitions for the festive season, and, of course, the array of high quality shopping on parade in the city centre for the buying of gifts. In a deliberate policy to widen, deepen and lengthen this period of festivities, the Council (with support from city centre stores) had sought to highlight that the religious festival of Christmas and the seeing in of the New Year on the eve of 31 December were merely examples of a number of celebrations and activities over this period. Running for its second year, this innovative policy recognised both the diverse population of the city, and the significant levels of spending which take place during 'festivals'. The promotion highlighted how, in recent times, the Council has led the country in its attempts to mainstream 'multiculturalism' through public art, ethnic quarters, ethnic forums and initiatives such as the Winterval festival. A direct response to criticisms of previous policies which lacked just such innovation in recognising the cultural and ethnic diversity of the city's population, the lampooning of Winterval in the national and regional media has put such 'mainstreaming' policies on the defensive once again.

Reaffirming the international enclave (and the denial of citizenship) Birmingham's recent history has been one of massive investment in the construction of a number of 'flagship' projects, such as the International Convention Centre and Symphony Hall (which recently hosted a G8 summit), Brindley Place (a major leisure development of clubs, pubs, restaurants, shops, offices and elite housing on the old canal basin), and the National Indoor Arena, all of which have contributed greatly to transforming Birmingham's reputation and image. These developments have placed the city on the world map both economically, in sectors such as events and conventions, and, almost as important, symbolically. Further, there is no doubt that such developments have contributed to the civic pride of many residents of Birmingham. Yet these developments have also been, quite rightly, criticised for their divisiveness.[1] To many, the flagship projects have created an elite international enclave within Birmingham city centre: a space for the national and international business/tourist class, which is increasingly divorced from its regional and local context. Thus, much has been written of the power and wealth of such spaces sitting cheek-by-jowl with areas containing some of the poorest residents not only of the city but of the UK.

To its credit, Birmingham City Council has recognised this argument and, as new rounds of investment take place in the city centre (Bull Ring redevelopment, Martineau Galleries, Millennium Point, Centre Point, Arena Central), it is explicitly aiming to train economically-excluded residents so that they may re-enter the labour market and gain from the new employment opportunities. On a positive note, one could argue that the pre-existing and fairly hegemonic 'trickle-down' model of tackling poverty is being 'oiled' through

---

1. See, for example, P. Loftman and B. Nevin, 'Prestige urban regeneration projects: socio-economic impacts', in A. J. Gerrard and T.R. Slater (eds), *Managing a Conurbation: Birmingham and its Region*, Brewin Books, Studley 1996.

the coupling of economic development and labour market measures. However, whilst this is laudable, one cannot help feel that recent - divisive - history is about to repeat itself. It is about to do so because of the (still) limited vision of the future city centre encapsulated in the new developments of Britain's tallest skyscraper, offices, new shopping malls and leisure facilities. A city is being made to show and entertain investors rather than for local people to live in.

What is seemingly being forgotten in the rush to reinvent the city centre is the most fundamental and historical function of city centres, namely as spaces of collective and participatory citizenship rather than just as shop windows and business stop-overs: focal points for meeting and greeting, debating, living and breathing, acting out a part in the life of your city. Whilst the flagship projects have been identified as economically exclusive, what is less recognised is their social exclusion of many citizens from major spaces in the city centre (except as low-paid service workers). Boosterist city centre regeneration takes place at the expense of day-to-day urban living. This type of regeneration involves divisive economic strategies, coupled with urbanisation as a cultural/aesthetic project with which only certain fragments of city populations can identify. More shopping malls, business facilities and millenarian exhibits will have limited relevance to many Birmingham residents' daily lives. Moreover, this exclusion is more subtle than the use of CCTV and private security guards to exclude bag ladies, the homeless, young people, and the 'simply suspect' from the glitzy new spaces of consumption: it is about the production of new 'cultural' spaces in the image of certain fragments of international capital and particular constellations of the population. Put another way, Symphony Hall is a magnificent arena, but waxing lyrical over the City of Birmingham Symphony Orchestra playing minority interest music is very much part of a particular cultural upbringing.

Globalisation and the distinctiveness of place: Birmingham as multicultural city

To bypass the exclusive atmosphere of redevelopment, we argue that Birmingham should be managed with socially inclusive and multiculturalist[2] policies to the

---

2. Following Patel (see *Soundings* 12), whilst we use the term 'multiculturalism' we do so in the spirit not only of 'multiple cultures' but rather more as contested hybrid cultures and community identities whose state of flux - around particular key moments - must be central to analysis and practice.

fore. Those who live in the city know of the diversity of peoples and ways of living that make the city what it is: Birmingham's multiculturalism simply is. Any story countering its hybridity misses the *lived* truth of the city. Hybridity is so embedded in the city's history that it is easily evident in the public spaces, schools, hospitals, homes, and different districts that comprise the city. Yet, as boosterist city centre regeneration continues apace, that hybridity becomes erased and packaged such that participation in the centre is uneven.

In an economic climate where the ruthless discourse of globalisation dominates, the competition between cities to make their mark on that world is getting forever fiercer. Aspirations to become the next global city, world city, or whatever, are widespread as city authorities attempt to become stopping-off points for global flows of capital and investment. Yet as globalisation proceeds apace, so we should realise that the processes which underpin globalisation are also very much about distinctiveness; as the choice of location widens so the final choice is ever more attuned to the particular characteristics of locations and places. One response is a massive expansion of place marketing and civic boosterism, as everywhere attempts to become somewhere.

Birmingham, too, is faced with this dilemma, but we believe it should play the game differently and play to the strengths of its people. The 1991 census highlighted that over 20 per cent (and growing) of the city's population comprised minority ethnic groups; in other words, the city can truly claim to be a multicultural city - as can few others in a world that is supposedly becoming increasingly transcultural. Yet this distinctiveness of Birmingham, its particular uniqueness in the world, still seems recognised and celebrated by only limited numbers. Certainly, up until the berated, but highly symbolic, Winterval promotion, one has struggled to see conceptions of multiculturalism as a positive governmental and economic advantage. It is this aspect of Birmingham which is most missing from the showpiece developments of the city centre: multicultural city, *yes*; multicultural city centre/brand image ... *no*. It may be argued that this is one element which explains the lack of a 'sense of belonging' to the city and its 'official transformation' on the part of many residents and communities. In other words, the flagship projects are neither an economic *nor a cultural* transformation of which they can feel part. The boosterist culture of past and future redevelopment is in denial of the diversity that takes place in Birmingham.

Things could possibly be different if the message of diversity and hybridity was taken on board and worked with. In the contemporary climate, one cannot blame the City Council in courting the likes of Hammerson (property developers) as the providers of significant investment in resource-strapped times; but one wonders if the true potentials of hybrid Birmingham can ever be recognised in such a strategy. For example, what would happen if we ran with an idea that the next headline regeneration of old retail or industrial space would be not a shopping centre or office block but a World Centre for Cultural Hybridity - a centre for training, education and creation of awareness about 'diversity and difference' in the world and its particular focus in Birmingham. This might appear as random pie in the sky, but such a suggestion goes beyond the narrow vistas of conferences, shopping and offices.

A first question is 'why Birmingham?' An easy response would be that if a Sealife Centre is appropriate to Birmingham, then anything is. But there is more to it than that: Birmingham has only ever been a city of hybridity. Based inextricably on the growth of the British Empire, people, goods and capital have flowed in every direction from all corners of the globe to bring the city to where it is today: hybridity is the local (and global) truth. All aspects of Birmingham's history are cut through with its global links, and today's population are a sign of this. Meaningful use of this, which reinscribes it in a bold and egalitarian way, goes beyond ethnic food quarters where our difference from each other is turned into a set main course; we have to think beyond the 'balti logic' which is now sweeping restaurants and convenience meal shelves of national supermarkets. The diversity of our different histories, abilities, practices and skills needs to be brought to the fore and inextricably identified with Birmingham and its region. A World Centre for Cultural Hybridity could explore, through education, exhibition and example, the multiplicities of Birmingham's history. This new vision should not just be about presenting local hybrid versions of Chineseness, Islam or Irishness: it should cut to the heart of British life and show how Anglo culture, even at its most corporate, is already hybrid and has depended throughout the modern age on peoples and practices from all over the world. The effect of such an institution could be to overcome the prejudices which reduce participation in the present city centre and inhibit an honest engagement with our multicultural selves. This, we believe, is a necessary step to break the cycle of divisiveness that haunts present urban-economic logic.

What if such a place were to be built? No need for 'positive discrimination' or the like, since its very basis is that it belongs to all and reflects the material reality of life in Birmingham. Unlike the ICC or Symphony Hall, which indirectly favour particular cultural classes of inhabitants and visitors, this project would state clearly that city building is about connection and inclusion. Further, it is attitude changes which will pave the way for Birmingham City Council to realise its aims of bringing meaningful and participatory economic activity to many economically-excluded residents of the city.

The project's wider cultural impact might begin to give people the confidence to enter the spaces of the city that they fear to tread through a 'lack of understanding', or a fear of 'not belonging'; to recognise the shared histories of the city. More residents of the city would recognise a cultural space in the city centre which was relevant to them, and of which they too could be proud when friends and relatives visit (from around the UK and world).

But where would the money come from? We are probably correct in assuming that property developers such as Hammerson (who are rebuilding the Bull Ring) are unlikely to show interest in such a scheme. But, remember, international capital is culturally diverse too. We are only now beginning to understand the dense and far-flung sets of trade links which a diverse city like Birmingham has within its borders, and has had for many years. It is these links which raise the possibility of calling on rarely tapped sources of major overseas investment - from the Middle East, south Asia, southern Africa, etc - *if* the scheme resonates with the cultural aspirations of segments of these (both international and local) communities. After all, who would have prophesied that Harrods and Fulham Football Club would be owned by an Egyptian? Elsewhere, the North East has Sir John Hall and, indeed, 'we' have our very own Richardson brothers. But in a diverse city, the Richardson brothers are only one of a number of possibilities. For example, Birmingham has been the recent recipient of the Pagoda - a gift to the city from the 'Overseas Chinese' businessman Wing Yip, aimed at reinforcing the presence of the Chinese community in Birmingham.[3]

Birmingham already is global

Fundamentally, this argument is about the ways in which Birmingham's

---

3. A recent estimate has put the combined economic output of the Overseas Chinese at close to $600 billion worldwide.

regeneration and image relates to the people who live in the city. Today, a major element of the reinvention of city centres is as internationally-recognised showcases for their cities. Yet the paradox of this promotion is that in achieving this goal many centres are becoming divorced from their cities and the people who live in them. Indeed, not only do they become merely the stopping-off point of an internationally mobile elite (complete with city checklists), but 'trickle-down economics' becomes a story of increased economic, social, cultural and political polarisation and exclusion. The point of this piece is to argue that Birmingham may have more possibilities than most to side-step this process. For the point is that *Birmingham already is global.* Its multiculturalness and diversity is its internationality. The ICC and its like may begin to draw on some of this in its cultural aspirations and symbolism, but there are as yet many other under-represented cultures which have long taken root in Birmingham. To draw on these may enable the meeting of aspirations both of international recognition *and* a city centre as a living, breathing heart of a vibrant multicultural city.

Concepts of 'place' are as pertinent today as ever; indeed, Birmingham's flagship boosterism has been precisely about the creation of one such view of place. But there has always been a question about who it is for whom we are creating this view, and at what expense? We have tried to outline an alternative version of city-building equally, if not more, global - a path of social and cultural investment drawing on the 'rooted globalisations' of Birmingham's population. For long after mobile capital has moved on, the residents of the city remain. As a political, economic and social message our argument goes wider than Birmingham, and wider than the growing list of 'wannabe' global cities.

We would like to acknowledge the encouragement and advice of Terry Slater, a long-time resident of Birmingham, in the production of this article.

The art of life

Jonathan Rutherford

With the breakdown of the old order, everyone is faced with the stark question of how to live.
Jonathan Rutherford *argues that we need an ethics of living.*

Despite historically unparalleled degrees of social stability and affluence, we are living through a period of profound change in our personal and emotional lives. Capitalism is transforming its own economic and geographical conditions which produced the old, work centred class categories. Globalisation, the emergence of new knowledge based, post-industrial sectors, and the expansion of the service economy have radically altered the time and rhythm of work. The end of empire, postwar new Commonwealth immigration, and the radical changes to family life and sexual values, are transforming the social character of English ethnicity. Individuals are being freed from the constraints of the old order, but the new opportunities have brought new risks which mirror the injustices of the old class society. Greater degrees of personal self-expression coincide with new forms of standardisation in which the rhetoric of the market - the supremacy of personal choice, the inviolability of individual ambition - disguises the disparate life chances of people. The dissolving of working-class ties has led to unprecedented degrees of inequality, intensifying the experience of poverty and creating new forms of social exclusion. We are, in the words of the German sociologist Ulrich Beck, entering a period of capitalism without class, in which collective relationships to the means of production have been radically disrupted by de-industrialisation and unregulated forms of wild capitalism. The old working-class cultures have fragmented and are unable to mobilise individuals against the new forms of risk they face, nor, in the main, can they generate a contemporary language of self affirmation and cultural empowerment. Their bonds of solidarity are now vestigial. There will be no revival of social democracy as we have known it, because the alliance of class interests which brought it into effect has disappeared.

Our increasing personal isolation in society has encouraged a greater emphasis on individuality, self-reliance, and the search for an ethics and practice of identity and emotional life. Dissatisfaction is expressed in our concern for the particular and everyday rather than in grand ideological themes. This absorption with the quality of life is a response to new antagonisms and problems which necessitate people's active engagement. For those in paid work, time has become a scarce commodity. Family life has lost its common temporal rhythm and spatial focus, and requires new skills of management, co-ordinating the competing needs, interests and activities of adults and children. People's expectations of relationships are growing. Sexuality has been politicised, and the body has been become the subject of ubiquitous forms of self management and modification. Personal appearance and self-presentation now embody valuable forms of social capital. The growing desire for the immaterial - rest, free time, friendship, fun, creative work - is encouraging a conflict with the work ethic, and new demands for personal and social well being. The meaning of life is the subject of countless self-help books. Established religions and old-fashioned notions of morality are challenged by new representations of the sacred, and by personal ethics and alternative spiritual beliefs. The things that matter to people are increasingly outside the instrumental, managerialist language of politics and the sphere of governance.

There is an argument that the contemporary search for authenticity in personal life is a defeat for civic virtue and democracy; that we are hovering on the fringes of a consumerist, privatised dystopia. It is true that the modern turn to the self coincides with public apathy towards local and national elections and a general lack of interest in politics. But as Adam Smith reminds us in *Wealth of Nations*, the realm of the public in modernity was originally secured by the market and the utility of money: 'everyman in some measure becomes a merchant'. Thus benevolence towards others was subordinated to the function of exchange value. If this instrumental and utilitarian culture of capitalism was contested and somewhat dissipated by the social solidarities created by the Second World War and the welfare state, it reasserted itself in the 1980s, and continues to be dominant. Neo-liberal capitalism has undermined forms of public authority and representative democracy through the process of individualisation, and its global, standardising, commodity culture.

But, paradoxically, it has extended democracy into cultural, personal and family life. A new relationship between the individual, the local and the global is emerging and it is here, not in the public realm of governance, that there is a re-evaluation of what an ethics of living might be, a search for a new vocabulary of virtue. The individual practice of identity-making, of negotiating relationships and defending oneself against the social forces of capital, racism and sexism, is not simply an aesthetic of lifestyle, but the necessary emotional work of everyday life. Concern with private life and the cultivation of the self is central to the revolution in cultural life of the late twentieth century. Contemporary preoccupations with intimacy, friendship, the meaning of life, death, love, family, belonging, sexuality, the body and emotions are prefigurative forms of culture; they are what Raymond Williams has described as 'structures of feeling': 'affective relations of consciousness and relationships: not feeling against thought, but thought as felt and feeling as thought'. [1] They are a part of emergent values and identities across Western Europe.

Protestantism and the individual

The preoccupation with the self, emotions and identity has been a central feature of the history of modernity, and has been closely affiliated to the constitutional struggle for civic democracy. In Europe, during the seventeenth century, the emergence of finance and trade capitalism increasingly directed the private economic activity of the family household towards the commodity market. This led to the establishment of a public realm of the trading and middle classes, and a separate domestic culture of family life. At the same time the Puritan revolution secured a sphere of private individual autonomy.

The Reformation had initiated an idea of human togetherness radically different from Catholicism, which had bound individuals to the church through their bodies and emotions. Protestantism promoted an imaginary community based on faith, which abstracted religion from people's everyday lives. The meaning of life was no longer fixed, but became a task of individual self-reflection and the examination and interpretation of God's word. Self-examination

1. Raymond Williams, 'Structures of Feeling' in *Marxism and Literature*, Oxford University Press 1978.

replaced oral confession and a Puritan culture of spiritual autobiographies, diary writing and personal testaments gave rise to a self-conscious, inner life of the individual. Sensuality was identified with the despotism of the Catholic church and the absolutism of the King. Protestantism was intent on ridding society of the baroque cultures and sacred communities which gloried in this divine earthly power. Emotions threatened the rational order of things. The sacred gradually came to reside in the mind rather than the body and community. The Protestant revolution marked the growth of a possessive individualism integral to the rise of capitalism. Individual identity came to express a person's place in the new order of things. When John Bunyan in *The Pilgrim's Progress* (1678) falls asleep and dreams a dream of Christian, 'a man clothed in rags', breaking out in his lamenting cry 'What shall I do?', he inaugurates a cultural revolution which symbolises the transition from traditional society. The narrative of early European modernity was this pilgrim's progress to his spiritual homeland; the transition from Providence and fate to the idea of personal destiny. But in the same instant he establishes a profound problem about the place of love, intimacy, and emotions in human life. Christian's despairing call to be saved is answered by Evangelist who tells him to follow 'yonder shining light'. Bunyan watches in his dream as Christian runs from his own door, his wife and children pleading with him to return, and he stops up his ears crying, 'Life, life, eternal life'. The ambivalence of choice: human love or divine grace.

In this pilgrim's progress, this transition to the idea of personal destiny, the religious ethic of righteousness was gradually surpassed by a pragmatism and psychology of selfhood. The Calvinist anxiety 'how can I be good?' became the secular 'how can I be happy?' The narrative of modernity was no longer leading towards a spiritual home but towards human perfection. The application of enlightenment values of reason and persuasion would achieve the long transition to a perfect society. With the emergence of science and a metropolitan public culture, the eighteenth century witnessed the secular development of the individual's inner life, and numerous social theories attempting to explain how a secular society was possible.

The philosopher David Hume was concerned with the conflict between reason and emotion, in particular with the sociability which bound individuals into a society. In *Treatise of Human Nature*, published in 1739-40, he argued that feelings permitted the expression of social bonds upon which society was founded. Sociability and moral values were inaugurated by the flow of emotions - sympathy - between people. Hume's language of sentiment and sensibility was challenged by his friend Adam Smith. He argued in *Theory of Moral Sentiments*, published in 1759, that unmediated emotions of sentiment usurped reasonable behaviour and undermined the ties which bound people together. To ensure the harmony of society, emotions could not be completely private and spontaneous but had to be learnt through social interaction. In Smith's *Theory*, the concept of sociability becomes a calculation of self-interest which distances the subject from both himself and from others: 'We must imagine ourselves not the actors, but the spectators of our own character and conduct'. By the time he had published *The Inquiry into the Nature and Causes of Wealth of Nations* in 1776, he had extended issues of human relatedness further still into political economy. Smith anchored morality and its regulation in the 'immense machine' of public life and government. Justice and the rule of law, not sociability, would be the ties which bound citizens to society. The public good would be managed by the 'invisible hand' of the market. Society, he argued, could manage without benevolence, though it would be, as a consequence, 'less happy'.

Romanticism

Of all the Enlightenment philosophers it was Rousseau who most successfully navigated a path between 'unreasonable rationalism' and 'superstitious anti-rationalism', between individualism and a recognition of democratic and egalitarian ideals. His introspection, his concern with the memory of childhood, and his search for personal fulfilment and disdain for authority, established a revolutionary fashioning of the self which has become a central feature of modernity. In the final decade of the eighteenth century, Rousseau's writing had a significant influence on English supporters of the French Revolution, and marked the birth of Romanticism.

Romanticism in England emerged out of the political agitation for constitutional reform between 1792 and 1796, and expressed the humanitarian sympathy associated with the French and American Revolutions. Romanticism was a continuation of the 'Age of Sensibility' and gave expression to an intense reaction against the rationalising tendencies of the Enlightenment and the anti-human, anti-aesthetic influences of commerce. It emphasised the inner life of the imagination, and sought through its depictions of nature a language of immanence. At least half of the literature published in England between 1780 and 1830 was written by women, but the growing cultural dominance of men in the early nineteenth century has concealed the central role women played in the romantic movement. More than this, it obscured how the making of the modern self and identity was a profoundly masculine affair, which reflected men's attempt to claim personal feeling as the authentic expression of the individual without succumbing to the sentimental emotions associated with women.

In *Emile*, published in 1760, Rousseau describes Emile's first real passion as his love for Sophie. 'Sophie you are the arbiter of my fate. You know it well. You can make me die of pain. But do not hope to make me forget the rights of humanity. They are more sacred to me than yours. I will never give them up for you'. Sophie is Rousseau's perfect imaginary wife, a coquette who is confined to the private realm and subordinated to the abstract, rational ideas of public life. 'Women have, or ought to have, but little liberty', he declared. 'What nonsense!' retorted Mary Wollstonecraft in A *Vindication of the Rights of Woman* (1792). 'Still harping on the same subject, you will exclaim', she writes to Gordon Imlay in 1795. 'How can I avoid it, when most of the struggles of an eventful life have been occasioned by the oppressed state of my sex: we reason deeply, when we forcibly feel' (letter 19). The feminism of Mary Wollstonecraft demanded women's right to reason and the demand for a public existence alongside men. Men cultivating their finer feelings were unwilling to admit women into public intellectual life. Similarly they were anxious in their exploration of the emotions. If women were the unreasonable creatures of sentiment then the feelings of men had to be marked out as separate, different and superior. The aesthetic of life which became known as Romanticism evolved not so much in the absence of women writers but in their exclusion by men intent on fashioning a language of feelings denuded of feminine connotations. The degeneration of the French revolution, and political reaction in Britain, encouraged the displacement of Romanticism's original humanitarian sympathy into a cultivation of the solitary genius. A man's expression of his sentiment was less for others than for the higher things of life. He could aspire to be free from social relations, to give birth to the idea of himself. Feelings were no longer Hume's expression of sociability, but increasingly belonged to the solitary world of the exceptional individual.

By the end of the century conservatives associated sentiment with the revolutionary benevolence of the French Revolution, and condemned it as a threat to the social order. Even radicals like the young Coleridge linked it with flighty female readers of the novel. What had been a mark of sincerity had become associated with foreigners and effeminacy. British national identity forged in the war with France was defining itself in its rejection of certain forms of emotional expression - abstract idealism, public displays of sentimental emotions, introspection - in favour of a sturdy, unreflecting manliness secured by the dispassionate, the provable and the measurable.

> 'British national identity was defining itself as sturdy, unreflecting manliness'

The late eighteenth century gave form to the political, social and cultural contours of European modernity: the cultural differences of femininity and masculinity; the emergence of empires and the racialising of European cultures; the conflict between reason and feelings, commerce and sensibility; the divide between the public and private spheres of social life; the creation of the modern self and its other as a defining category of social life. Romanticism developed as a counterculture of modernity, establishing a tradition of opposition to the utilitarianism of capitalism through its promotion of the authenticity of emotional life, its appeal to nature, and, with the rise of agnosticism, a belief in the sublime. But it too was subjected to its own counter culture, not only in the writing of women and the emergence of feminism but in the narratives of former slaves who exposed its complicity with imperialism and the emerging discourses of racism. Ignatius Sancho, who was born in 1729 on a slave ship, and who became a friend of the sentimental novelist Laurence Sterne, wrote his best selling *Letters* with the intention of proving that an African possessed the same abilities as a European. Published in 1782, two years after his death, they attracted 1200 subscribers. Olaudah Equiano, the first political leader of Britain's black community, similarly wrote a best selling life story *The Interesting Narrative* (1789). These narratives exposed the way in which commerce reduced human life to goods and chattels, and how the racialised character of sensibility all too frequently failed to extend its benevolence to black people. In its darker aspect, the immanence of Romanticism was subsumed into the absolutism of an authentic truth of the self, which provided the chief ideologies of the nineteenth and twentieth centuries - nationalism, racism, fascism and Marxism - with their respective aesthetic and philosophical justifications. At the heart of these ideologies was the longing to implement the utopian desire for human completeness, a pursuit of perfection which required the total rationalisation of human conduct. Marx in the *1844 Manuscripts*, drawing on German Romanticism, attempted to address what it means to be human, to describe the ways in which the commodity relations created by capitalism alienated the worker from himself. Behind his description of alienation lay Hegel's belief in an underlying unity of human essence and world, the notion of the inevitable unfolding of history towards human perfection. Marxism and its dialectic of historical materialism was the legacy of the Enlightenment's unreasonable belief in reason. In the hands of Lenin, it differed little from the punishing theology of Calvinism. One demanded the surrender of life to god, the other of life to the state and history.

The collapse of Communism was the most recent rout of the Enlightenment project of human perfection through the application of reason and science. In contrast, other traditions of English/British socialism - the Socialist League of William Morris, Edward Carpenter's brand of romantic socialism, the New Left and the social movements of the 1960s - have been sceptical of modernity's rationalising ethos and derived their languages from native Romanticism. They fostered a creative engagement with the world, antipathetic to the bureaucratic didacticism of the Fabians, the industrial ethos of Labour, and the scientism of theoretical Marxism. Their emphasis on emotions and inner experience, and the search for an authentic self, enabled a democratising of personal life, and redefined the boundaries of political discourse. But these traditions of collectivism also have not been saved from history. They too were a product of the culture of puritanism. Their notions of human solidarity were invented by the religious traditions of the non-conformists, and they harboured a moralism and a politics of judgmentalism which became evident in their suspicion of popular culture, and their prescriptive attitudes towards lifestyle and personal opinion. At one time it was religious authority and bourgeois propriety which rewarded the masses for being dutiful, emotionally restrained, self denying, or deferential. Now that people have rejected the imposition of this class authority, this form of left politics, like its religious forebears, has also been dispersed by secular individualism.

An ethical politics

Today there are no more utopias, and no more dreams of brotherhood. The sign we live under is one which is ambivalent in its own meaning. It was Jacques Derrida who theorised this unending slippage of language, the impossibility of securing meaning; Jean Francois Lyotard who described our modern predicament of identity as always arriving at our destination too soon or too late. In such a culture we are left to our own devices - adrift for the moment, but also free to take ethical decisions. There is no left any more, in the sense of an identifiable moral and political authority - only the remnants of a number of antagonistic traditions. There is no future in attempting to repair and impose one of the old ideologies, to homogenise difference, or try and stem the leaking away of identity. But equally there is little to be gained by pretending they never existed. A future politics will be fashioned in the present on the basis of the past. What then are we to do? It is a question which haunts the texts of the European left. It is the spectre which besets this moment of modernity, because unlike the puritans, or for that matter Lenin, we no longer believe in the Celestial City where the streets are paved with gold. As Marx accurately predicted, the logic of capitalism encourages the breaking up of human ties and a more intensive commodifying of everyday life. The response of the market is to promote the personal realisation of the few, rather than social and moral concern for all, but there is no human respite guaranteed in the allure of profit, or the individual pursuit of wealth. Adam Smith informed his readers over two hundred years ago that commodity relations will never lead to personal fulfilment or happiness. And Marx, sixty-eight years later, perversely insisted that the 'goal of the economic system is the unhappiness of society'. In the Romantic era love became the great melodrama which would beat back the dull, patriarchal world of duty and emotional impoverishment. It was the beacon of liberation which would launch the lives of its young protagonists into the future of their dreams. The secular religion of love was invented, and this has now become ordinary, the stuff of everybody's dreams. It still holds the promise of transforming our lives, of connecting us in deep and enduring ways to other human beings. Love is an emancipation which enables us to be present in our own lives. But the Romantic tradition, in its rejection of the fractured and instrumental relations of capital, longs for a holistic and organic culture, and this lends it a deep and abiding fear of cultural and racial difference. Love cannot be the basis for a politics for it tends to reduce difference to sameness. We need an ethics of virtue. To learn to be with oneself in the presence of other people is how the philosopher Emmanuel Levinas describes ethical practice. We are not wholly alone in the world, nor are we part of a totality to which all others belong. Our encounter with others who are not reducible to ourselves, and the realisation that we must negotiate sharing the world with them, is the moment ethical life begins.

I t is this encounter with otherness in the contemporary democratisation of culture, family and personal life which will provide a future vocabulary of political radicalism in the industrialised world. It will not be another singular ideology of anti-capitalism, but one which holds the potential for becoming various, a counterculture of modernity able to address the proliferation and dispersal of contemporary social and political antagonisms. The development of such a politics cannot begin with defining strategies, agencies or ideologies. In a post-scarcity society in which economic determinants play a less significant role in determining the fate of a majority of its citizens, the more functionalist forms of politics and sociology are no longer able to explain individual motivations and behaviour, nor do they have the language for representing people's aspirations for a better life. A beginning can be made by returning to the old question appropriated by religion. What does it mean to be alive? And with the memory of slavery, and the barbarism of European Fascism, Nazism and Communism - not to mention current forms of ethnic cleansing and racism - this leads to a further, political, question. What is the relationship of human life to sovereign power? Such an ethical politics requires a cultural and intellectual life which follows the spirit of Levinas' Jewish humanism, reading against the grain, interpreting rather than prescribing and legislating, placing questions at the heart of the search for identity and meaning.

It was the late Michel Foucault who recognised that such a philosophy returns us to the early Stoics and their art of living. At the beginning of the first millennium, Seneca, in his essay 'On The Shortness of Life', wrote 'But learning how to live takes a whole life, and, which may surprise you more, it takes a whole life to learn how to die.' As Foucault points out in his book *Care of the Self*, the Stoic concern with the cultivation of the self - 'spend your whole life learning how to live' - was not simply a valorisation of private individualism, but indicative of a crisis of the subject: 'the difficulty in the manner in which the individual could form himself as an ethic of the subject'. Norbert Elias has described the changes in the customs of the Roman upper classes and how subsequent legislation altered the balance of power between men and women in women's favour.[2] It was this weakening of private patriarchal authority and the changing relationship between the family household and the public sphere of the state which encouraged a philosophy of care of the self. Elias argues that a central factor in fostering more egalitarian relations between men and women was the role of the state in protecting the person, property and income of women. He concludes, 'the same holds true, I think, in our time.'

I t is the paradox of an ethical politics centred on the individual that it can only develop through new forms of social solidarity. In issue 12, *Soundings* addressed this question in Bernard Latour's argument for a politics of coexistence (*Ein Ding ist ein Thing*), and in the practices of transversal politics described by Cynthia Cockburn, Lynette Hunter and Nira Yuval-Davis. Today it is necessary to live without guarantees but nevertheless with an ethical framework that acknowledges co-dependency, and that care of the self and the pursuit of self-interest is intrinsically bound to care of others and concern for society. 'If you wish to be loved: love' wrote the Stoic philosopher Seneca to his 'pupil' Lucilius. In an age of secular individualism in which, for many in the West, the dread of loneliness and fear of failure have replaced the apprehension of hunger and disease, there is a need to cultivate new representations of human commonality and the pleasures of being alive, to invent a language of virtue - notions of goodness which are pragmatic and contingent and not a pious observance of the Law. In the past these were expressed in religious symbols and spaces of the sacred. They were timeless, changeless representations of a pre-modern, homogeneous culture, and an undifferentiated world view which contributed to ethnic and religious barbarism. The search for a new settlement between the individual and society requires the invention of plural, non-absolutist and deinstitutionalised forms, objects, languages and spaces in which our inner being finds an emotional identification with the world beyond, and which fosters coexistence with the others who occupy it.

We can never know the truth of ourselves, we will never achieve immanence or attain transcendence. We can only ever get hold of the world indirectly

---

2. Norbert Elias, 'The Changing Balance of Power between the Sexes - A Process-Sociological Study: The Example of the Ancient Roman State', in *Theory Culture and Society* Vol. 4, 1987.

through representation in language. We also are made in language. It makes us, as well as the world. The sacred is simply a metaphor for the excess of world over word. The left died when it failed, imaginatively, creatively, aesthetically and politically, to help us in this act of knowing and reparation. Life is a work, and it is the emotional and intellectual business of politics to invent new languages which redescribe the world and help us live in it better and with pleasure. If we live today with personal insecurity, and our commonwealth has a paucity of public languages, it is within human natures to reach for something more which is beyond us, to grasp for words which will correspond to what is missing. Out of this ethical activity can emerge a renewed collective impulse for economic justice, personal emancipation and political democracy.

This is a shortened version of an essay which will appear in Art of Life, *edited by J. Rutherford, Lawrence and Wishart, April 2000.*

Experiences of strangeness
Angela McRobbie

Kevin Davey, *English Imaginaries*, Lawrence and Wishart, £12.99

This book is an attempt to correlate a number of diverse figures in the field of what Davey calls the Anglo-British imaginary, all of whom have an oblique, or let us say uneasy relation with the more stable core of English identity. Their position - both inside and at odds with the canonic tradition of English modernity - makes them particularly interesting figures today. Davey sees them as demonstrating a key principle which he argues is necessary for us if we are to avoid the dangers of the new nationalisms. This is the principle of strangeness and of being a stranger, with the ability to communicate the value of living within a community of strangers. Davey sees in these figures some of the values he wants to fully acknowledge, 'improper behaviour ... sexual experiment and downright bad-tempered dissent'.

He draws on the important work of the French psychoanalyst Kristeva, who argues that forms of national identification are based on processes of abjectification. The other is spewed out, like vomit, an object of revulsion. She does not, as Davey reminds us, look to a better time when abjection no longer exists, but instead encourages recognition of abjection (horror and revulsion) as within ourselves: 'instead of searching for a scapegoat in the foreigner ... I must try to tame the demons that are in me'. Kristeva seems to be suggesting that if we were all to internalise something of the quality of being a foreigner, that would in itself dissipate the angry projections of otherness. We are all, by necessity, foreigners to ourselves. Davey in turn shows how a number of writers, artists and musicians dotted about the landscape of English culture draw on and explore their own different experiences of being abject, that is the object of horror or revulsion.

He makes it clear that he is not proposing a kind of counter-tradition of political radicalism, although at points it seems that the Anglo-British counter-culture of modernity he describes invokes not only Gilroy's seminal account in the *Black Atlantic* but also carries memories of Raymond Williams's *Culture and Society*. But this fruitful uncertainty, this sense that the figures he offers the reader in some peculiar way open up avenues of thought which resonate with ambivalences of identity and belonging, and also prise apart the security of a stable democratic tradition, also accounts for some of the problems in the book. I shall come back to these in a moment.

It is important to note that the author is not only drawing on the psychoanalytic perspective of Kristeva. He also draws (albeit critically) on Gramsci's writing on the national popular, and on his discussion on the historical conjuncture. A sharp sense of history is thus brought to bear on these diverse figures, from Nancy Cunard to Pete Townshend to Mark Wallinger. Three further themes wind their way through the book. First there is the presence of blackness in the white imaginary and its counterpart, the experience of whiteness in the black imaginary. These are considered in Davey's essays on Cunard, and writer and poet David Dabydeen. The second theme is the particular relation of state and nation in modern Britain, and the third is the recent modernisation of this configuration undertaken by new Labour, which found cultural expression in the Cool Britannia episode of 1998.

The first essay, on Nancy Cunard, describes the life and work of this heiress who in the 1920s turned her back on the landed gentry and the world of London salons, to become instead a 'modernist icon'. She wrote what appears to have been undistinguished poetry, lived in France, embraced the Africanism of aesthetic modernism and then the combination of left politics and surrealist art represented by figures like Aragon, Breton and others. Davey argues that this phase of globalisation - 'of tourism and travel, of literary markets, and the de-territorialised habitus of an ejected Anglo-British elite' - has the effect of making England's hegemony less assured. This was, he continues, a moment of transfiguration for women like Cunard and also homosexual men. Cunard continues her journey of transgression by taking a series of black lovers, including George Padmore, and going on to edit the influential anthology *Negro*. She was also an alcoholic and died after being confined to a mental asylum in England in 1964.

The first among several questions raised by this account is how right Davey is in positing Cunard in this role of disturbing the racialised and sexual psyche of England. Did she really shake its composure and its grandeur? Certainly she played an important role in promoting the European avant garde, and the advent of modernism. But her wealth protected her from material suffering, while her gender produced, I would say, that sad loneliness of the bohemian woman, the woman of modernity, the mistress and lover who moves aimlessly from man to man in a twilight world of alcohol. Jean Rhys experienced this same historical moment and also its wasteland-like sadness, but her writing shines on. Nancy Cunard was simply not that important.

This same uncertainty as to whether or not Davey's chosen figures do fulfil the role he posits for them carries on through the book. J. B. Priestley clearly does offer a voice of dissent from those socialists in favour of the strong state. He is also at odds with the post-war Labour Party while still retaining a kind of local or regional socialism. But Davey's account here is possibly his least convincing portrait. In the case of Pete Townshend, guitarist with The Who and proponent of London Mod style and Pop Art, Davey argues his performances 'mobilise the somatic and re-enact the traumas of identification, reliving the pain of separation … rendering his own body abject'. In short, Davey is describing a certain mode of masculine vulnerability articulated by Townshend through a working-class identity and a positioning within pop commercial culture rather than high art. However at points he overstates his case to impress upon the reader the cogency of his argument as a whole. It's quite possible to examine the work and figure of Townshend in sociological terms without entering into the field of his 'separation anxiety and rage against the … inauthenticity of identification'. Davey expends too much intellectual energy in unpicking the motives of Townshend who in recent years has been working with the Princes Trust and has thus 'loaned the cultural assets of Mod … to the modernising wing of monarchy'. Without running the risk of anti-intellectualism, it is perhaps also simply the case that Townshend, an ex-alcoholic and a man interested in disadvantaged youth, decided this was a way he could be useful.

With Westwood, my dialogue with Davey opens out to straightforward disagreement. The recent biography of Westwood reveals her to be politically well to the right, and intellectually almost completely reliant for her speeches and other interventions on a reactionary, upper-class aesthete who she has paid to give her private tuition for years. This is not to dispute the suggestion that her fashion design displays a fascination with national identity, monarchy, and its subversion. But to me Westwood reveals her instinctively unpleasant politics in her comments about the Spice Girls as 'animals without style'. The final two essays in the book are a good deal more convincing. The review and analysis of the work of Guyanese-British writer Dabydeen demonstrates his concern with re-visiting British history through the images and writing of Hogarth and Turner. I would have thought Dabydeen to be an influence on the black artist Yinka Shonibare in this strategy of asking the white British to look again upon themselves with a new sense of the strangeness of their own historical endeavours. 'Let white people make the effort to be mongrel', as Dabydeen puts it. Finally the essay on the artist Mark Wallinger stands out from the others for the reason that the exposition of his complex re-working of the oil painting tradition of Stubbs and his version of Englishness is immediately clear. Consequently there is none of the effort needed in some of the other essays to twist the work to fit with the argument; instead it is simply revealed in the course of Davey's discussion. Despite these reservations, this is a valuable book. It opens out a new and imaginative field for exploring the relations between the nation state and dissonant cultural practices.

Feminisms old and new
Alyson Pendlebury

Natasha Walter (ed), *On the Move: Feminism for a New Generation*, Virago
Natasha Walter, *The New Feminism* Virago
Germaine Greer, *the whole woman*, Doubleday

On the Move, edited by Natasha Walter, is a collection of essays and interviews which considers what feminism means to women in the late 1990s. The contributors come from a variety of backgrounds; some are teenagers and others are professional women, writers and broadcasters.

All the young women interviewed (whose ages ranged from 15 to 18) considered themselves feminists, but disliked the 'radical lesbian' image which they associate with feminism. They preferred to define feminism on their own terms, as the pursuit of equality for women, both at home and at work. All felt that marriage is the best environment for raising children, and anticipated that their husbands would take an equal share in the domestic chores. This expectation was often based on their own experience. One cannot help feeling, however, that as these young women grow older, their optimism will be tempered somewhat by the reality of women's continuing inequality and impoverishment. A short story in the book, 'Lentils and Lilies', by Helen Simpson, illustrates this, contrasting the optimism of the young woman who has grown up to expect equality with the view of the older woman with children who finds herself unsupported by her partner or the state, and struggles to cope.

Women are a diverse group, and one of the difficulties facing feminists is how to achieve unity whilst acknowledging this diversity. Jenny McLeod describes the white liberal feminist preoccupation with equality as too narrow to answer the needs of black women, who also have to deal with racism, and its impact on their relationships with men. She argues that, rather than reacting to racism in a self-destructive way, second generation black women are becoming more assertive, and as a result, the gender politics of black heterosexual relationships are changing rapidly. Stephanie Theobald calls for a revival of lesbian feminism, and attacks the trivialisation of lesbian sexuality in the media and the emergence of the chic lesbian and the bi-curious female.

Julie Bindel has found the media an unexpected ally, through which radical feminist ideas have entered the mainstream. One of the drawbacks of feminism's mainstream position, however, is a reluctance to analyse sexual politics, and Katherine Viner discusses the worrying trend whereby women who have enjoyed media success are complicit in their own degradation as sexual commodities. The example she uses is that of Ulrika Jonsson, who in May 1998 appeared in *Loaded* magazine wearing manacles. Such willing participation in women's objectification indicates that male approval is more important to women than female approval, presumably because this is where power resides, and Viner argues that this represents a greater expression of male power over women than that found in pornography. The personal is still political, because now women who want to consider themselves sexual beings feel pressure to agree to anything that is demanded of them.

Other contributors focus on party politics. Helen Wilkinson describes Margaret Thatcher as a powerful role model, arguing that while feminists procrastinated she broke new ground for women in politics. In contrast to this, Oona King sees Thatcher as the exception which proves the rule that women continue to have unequal access to power in Britain. Government policies still assume that women will do the unpaid work of caring within families, although a practical, legislative feminism is emerging under New Labour. Given equal access, women will become equal, and will thereby bring more 'feminine' values into government and society. Aminatta Forna, however, argues that successful women who have been empowered by the efforts of past feminists now seem to reject activism, and without a revitalised feminism government policy is unlikely to change.

Walter's own book, *The New Feminism*, aims to present that revitalised feminism, and to suggest ways in which equality might be achieved in the twenty-first century. Feminism has become a central force in women's lives, but it lacks the unity which is necessary in order to instigate some of the fundamental changes she calls for. Walter argues that unity can be achieved by focusing solely on equality, and advocates a separation between the personal and the political, on the grounds that, 'It is simply wishful thinking on the part of past feminists to think that we could radically change the balance of power by changing the way women speak, or dress, or make love.' She argues that the feminism of the 1970s and 80s focused on the effects of oppression in women's private lives, thereby keeping women's attention on the traditional 'private sphere' of home, body, sexuality, and relationships. Her contention is that feminism must let its children 'grow up', and enjoy being women. She argues that the female 'love of physical culture', of dressing and making up, is not necessarily demeaning; rather it is simply a 'game', in which women may or may not choose to participate. Yet women's magazines do not reflect any alternatives to playing the beauty game, and those who do not want to participate are likely to feel profoundly alienated by the lack of content and sheer volume of advertising and 'beauty features' in women's publications.

One thing which does seem apparent from women's magazines is that women are becoming far more articulate about their sexuality, and it is here that the didacticism of past feminism is felt to be most inappropriate.

According to Walter, women do not need to be told how to have sex because the sexual battle is now between equals, and sexual power and vulnerability are transferable, with men and women alternating as 'victim' and 'oppressor'. The effects of pornography, Walter argues, depend upon the context in which it is viewed, and women should acknowledge their darker sexual desires, rather than simply projecting these onto men.

Women want privacy in their private lives and equality in their public lives, and the 'new feminism' will be materialist, since it is economic inequality which links all women across class and political divides. Suggested strategies for achieving equality include the reorganisation of working life, and a shift from the expectation of a 'linear' career path towards a more 'cyclical' working pattern for both sexes. A free national childcare network would enable lone mothers to escape from poverty, and parents taking a career break could be paid a statutory allowance by the state. It is suggested that these developments could be funded by raising the retirement age to seventy, an increase which would be mitigated by the proposed career breaks. Aside from childcare provision, women do not need special consideration, but equal access to power. The new feminism will focus on the public rather than the private 'sphere', and seek equality through legislative and political change.

By contrast, in the whole woman, Germaine Greer is not so much concerned with creating a new feminism as reminding readers that the issues identified by the 'old' feminism have still not been fully addressed, and that women's position has in some ways worsened. In what she describes as the 'false dawn of feminism', the notion of 'femininity' has become increasingly fake, with women's bodies being artificially altered in order to approximate male sexual fantasies. Naomi Wolf's statement that women have become the 'political ruling class' is swiftly and effectively discredited through a reminder of the extent of harassment and discrimination which women still face. Such optimism is shown to have been premature.

The book is divided into four main sections: 'body', 'mind', 'love' and 'power'. The 'body' section describes the extent to which the medical establishment controls women through their bodies, whether through cosmetic surgery or the trend for hysterectomy, and discusses attempts made by women to assert control over their own bodies, through self-starvation and mutilation. Despite its array of statistical information, the book is immensely readable, and by turns both serious and irreverent. The 'mind' section inexorably returns to the body, as this is both the focus of most women's anxieties - about health, shape, age, fertility, and sexual attractiveness - and the means by which they are controlled. Western societies seek to impose this anxiety about women's bodies upon the so-called developing world, with female genital mutilation (FGM) attacked as 'barbaric' by a society which performs unnecessary surgery on women as a matter of course. Greer is not condoning FGM, but attacking the hypocrisy of Western cultures with regard to the notion of the sacrosanct 'whole woman', whose labia may be intact but whose empty womb is considered a 'problem' best dealt with by removal. The whole woman is a woman who does not consider her body to be defective, does not believe that her womb is a 'void' inside her, and can age without fear of coming under surgical or hormonal attack from the medical establishment. She is liberated rather than equal, and, as yet, remains an ideal rather than an actuality (for part of Greer's message is that no woman escapes the negative images of womanhood with which she is confronted).

This book does the very necessary work of identifying and detailing the innumerable ways in which women remain unequal, and the centrality of the female body as battleground. Despite the feminist rhetoric with which the medical establishment trumpets Hormone Replacement Therapy, cervical screening, and fertility treatments, technology has been used to alienate women from their natural bodies. HRT adds even more menstrual cycles to a woman's life, cervical screening is unreliable, and ovarian hyperstimulation can be life-threatening. Motherhood has become fragmented into the genetic, gestational, and parental, and Greer suggests that ultimately, technology will dispense with women as childbearers altogether. To me, this seems unlikely, however: this is work currently being done for free, and technology is expensive. In addition, if, as Greer seems to imply, the notion of women as subordinates is inherent in male self-definition, men are unlikely to want to give this up. If technology rendered women obsolete, who, then, would men oppress? There can be little satisfaction to be gained from oppressing an artificial womb-environment rather than a real woman. What seems more probable is that invasive control over pregnancy and childbirth will increase, and women will be afforded even less dignity and respect in this role than they have at present. In her discussion of magazines aimed at teenagers, Greer shows that 'girl power' is just another case of women emulating men, whilst simultaneously conforming to masculinist fantasies. As she observes, 'The language of independence conceals utter dependence upon male attention, represented as difficult for a girl to get and all but impossible for her to keep.' Women, it is suggested, could perhaps learn to feign, if not feel, the same indifference towards male company and approval which men display towards women, and thereby avoid the humiliating role of the constant seeker of male attention. In what sounds like a return to 1970s segregationism, Greer suggests that women and men may be incompatible, and that in the future women will live in extended groups, with older women helping with childcare.

Running through the book is a muted call for a more socialist feminism. This emerges most clearly in the final section, entitled 'liberation', in which Greer attacks 'the world-wide feminization of poverty' and the unnecessary deprivation caused by late twentieth-century capitalism. Lifestyle feminists are warned that the 'next feminism' may come from the developing world, and since what links all women is shared discrimination and relative poverty, it is this which must be addressed. If women simply emulate the divisive values of 'masculinity' and term it 'equality' they are helping to perpetuate an already cruel and exploitative world-order, in which women and children are the main sufferers. Greer argues that women are not the same as men, and to emulate masculine behaviour in the name of equality is to become as miserable and restricted by the concept of 'masculinity' as men are, but with even less chance of living up to its demands. Men, too, need to be liberated, and it is women who will set the example. In this way, perhaps, men will eventually emulate women, but this cannot happen until the whole woman has become aware and proud of her potency and has found a way of expressing it.

Perhaps the most problematic part of the book for younger feminists will be the author's rather bleak view of sexual behaviour. Millennium sex, she argues, is pornography, the flight from women which makes both sexes lonely, and some people, usually men, rich. Greer describes abortion as a consequence of oppression and the heterosexual emphasis on penetrative sex, and suggests that all the pain and guilt caused by abortion could be avoided by shifting the emphasis away from intromission, viewed as an act of domination, with the behaviour of animals cited as evidence. Yet humans are not the same as animals in every way, and successful and loving relationships between men and women are possible, in which intercourse may be considered an act of union, rather than domination. Despite Greer's view, many women will feel they have made some progress in their sexual relations with men, and are not likely to appreciate the suggestion that this is delusional. We may have a long way to go, but we have gained some ground.

Greer's book offers women a timely reminder of the subtleties of their continuing oppression, and she presents this information with insight and humour. But one of the problems with her feminism is that it does not seem to have adapted to the changes of the last thirty years. The segregationist and socialist themes in her writing are likely to alienate younger feminists rather than win their support, as is the suggestion that women should change their sexual behaviour. However naively optimistic it may seem, the trend among younger feminists is towards attacking the legislative and political obstacles to women's equality, and keeping the personal personal.

Earthquakes, fires and lions
Andy Wallis

Mike Davis, *Ecology of Fear: Los Angeles and the Imagination of Disaster*, Picador

Mike Davis's seminal 1990 book *City of Quartz* left its reader with a vision of Los Angeles as a city teetering on the brink of collapse, a police state awash with state-of-the-art surveillance techniques. Writing to provoke and induce debate, Davis continually attempts to expose the hidden underbelly of a Los Angeles that is ridden with social, economic and political inequalities. What he succeeds in is in presenting a discourse that constantly manoeuvres between disciplines, one that is accessible to both the academic and the citizen. An avid socialist, he can appear angry, bitter and scathing, yet he has a style that is continually embellished with witticisms, a sense of 'justice' and intellectual rigour. What is so enticing about much of his work is the sense that he is a man who is genuinely passionate and concerned about the city and spaces he lives in: one who believes that social, cultural and ideological change is possible in a city that 'in the most profound sense, is suffering a crisis of identity'.

With the publication of his latest book *Ecology of Fear: Los Angeles and the Imagination of Disaster*, Davis continues his exploration of the hidden and secret aspects of Los Angeles. In the first five chapters of the book, Davis examines the various types of 'natural' disasters that have struck Southern California, arguing that they have, through various means, either been 'covered up' or have increased the inequalities in the city. In the penultimate chapter he traces these aspects of disaster through a narrative of LA based literature, and in the final chapter offers a glimpse of what the future in Los Angeles may look like. It is an exhaustive and extensive body of research that has already provoked much debate in the United States. Davis's central claim is that what Los Angeles has been experiencing throughout the twentieth century is a series of disasters that have been rendered invisible by individuals in positions of power and control, perpetuating the vision of Los Angeles as the sunshine city. It is this blindness and fog, he argues, that has actually encouraged disasters to occur in an apocalyptic environment. Davis claims that what has emerged from this ideological framework is a whole ecology that mixes and interconnects culture, society, politics and the environment.

In the opening chapter 'The Dialectic of Ordinary Disaster' Davis charts the effects earthquakes have had upon the economic and social structure of LA, arguing that these natural disasters have become political in terms of the mutual assimilation of economic circumstances and environmental concerns. What has occurred in Los Angeles is a shift from concerns over urban disasters (for example the Watts rebellion that Davis discussed so eloquently in *City of Quartz*) towards a fear of natural or possibly divine disasters, resulting in a middle-class exodus from Los Angeles' enclaved suburbs to cities such as Seattle. This shift has had devastating consequences in terms of the economic and social structure of the city. Through a lack of knowledge, or acknowledgement, of the effects of earthquakes upon urban development, real estate investors have peddled more money into the process of recovery than into prevention. Davis illustrates this in terms of the effect the Northridge earthquake had upon the urban poor in 1992 (the same year as the LA Uprisings), a disaster that was to be the most expensive in US history and one which the Clinton administration was quick to spend on, yet not to the benefit of the urban underclass. Davis claims that what is required to 'prevent' such disasters is a full understanding of the environment, and a plan to model the city accordingly, rather than short-term solutions for a space that is always waiting for the Big One.

Davis traces this historical neglect in the second chapter entitled 'How Eden Lost Its Garden', arguing that 'cover ups' or veilings of the natural disasters that are characteristic of the Los Angeles physical geography, have perpetuated both the fears and the actualities of environmental catastrophes. This process of creating a fog is perhaps most succinctly illustrated in another chapter where Davis discusses how tornadoes have struck Los Angeles throughout its historical development. He argues that during the years of 'boosterism', real estate developers and the media continually disguised the tornadoes that struck LA as either 'strong storms' or 'freak occurrences'. Davis exposes the secret natural history of LA to emphasise the fact that business, leisure and tourism have continually been at the top of Los Angeles' agenda at the expense of the truth that LA has had more incidences of tornadoes than Oklahoma City. What has occurred is a blatant disregard for the forces of nature in the name of progress and commerce.

The difficulty in defining the rural/urban dialectic is taken a step further in an analysis of how the urban has grown into the wilderness and vice versa through the threat of mountain lions and other wildlife. As the city has expanded into the mountainous terrain that surrounds Los Angeles, nature has also encroached upon the developed spaces of suburbia. Echoing sensibilities that Davis discussed in *City Of Quartz*, he argues that a middle-class paranoia and fear has emerged, through mountain lions invading the privileged and private spaces of gated communities, whereby the animals have the potential to physically harm the residents and are personified as street gang members. This further illustrates real estate developers' egotistical desire to control the rural without understanding the ecological effects of such economic processes. Combating this, the wildlife of the mountains has adapted itself to survive in the urban battlefield, accentuating the media-induced fears within these fortresses.

The theme of the uneven distribution of power is reflected in the responses of the authorities to fire. Davis argues that the fires that have occurred in tenement housing in Downtown LA (which have caused 119 deaths in the twentieth century) have gone largely unnoticed. The media and developers have concentrated their energies and resources on documenting, rebuilding and financially securing the privatised area of Malibu (a high fire-risk zone), rather than fire prevention in areas of in poor housing. For example, in 1993 two fires broke out within two weeks of each other: one in the movie star-ridden environment of Malibu, and another in a Downtown motel. The death tolls in these fires were identical, yet there was a mass invasion of fire fighters in Malibu and, significantly, 'none' for the disaster that affected the motel. Davis argues that mass suburbanisation has created a 'fire boom', and that these occurrences could be prevented if housing had not been built on a landscape susceptible to wild fires. Many fires could be prevented if the funds allocated to fire safety were made available to the poorer areas of the city.

It is in the final chapter 'Beyond Blade Runner' that Davis is most comfortable and cogent. He offers an apocalyptic vision of future LA and fully engages with the notion of fear being emblematic of the city's social ecology. Davis argues that the 1992 rebellion exposed the social injustices inherent within LA. Drawing upon familiar Davis themes such as surveillance, the racial Other, fortification and the decline and militarization of any 'real' public space, he argues that the rebellion was the inevitable outcome of an urban space built on segregation and fear: 'The 1992 riots vindicated the foresight of Fortress Downtown's designers. While windows were being smashed throughout the old business district, Bunker Hill lived up to its name'. Davis views the lack of welfare spending in downtown and the emergence of containment zones as being symptomatic and emblematic of the paranoid city of the future, creating a whole ecology that is already taking shape. What is required, Davis argues, is a change in and redistribution of the procession of power, whereby the environment and the social are juxtaposed to create an ontological understanding of the fabric of the city.

My main concern with Davis's book is that, although it is exhaustive in its research, it appears to be a documentation of 'hidden' facts rather than a full examination of what can, and needs to, be done. This is perhaps most explicit when he discusses the history of disaster literature and film based in LA. Rather than providing a full and critical analysis of these mediums and genres, Davis has a tendency to list. Although the texts he chooses present a fictional picture of current LA and justify his methodology, there is very little commentary regarding the effect these have had upon the city at large. This is repeated in the chapter discussing mountain lions, where there is a laborious historical analysis of hunting as sport, and of the transformation of the animal landscape. Although valid, such passages do at times disrupt the trajectory of the narrative, making it a bible of facts and figures rather than a critique of this emerging ecology.

Another criticism I have is that while Davis is seen as a radical figure and as one who exposes the corruption and lies of those in control, he pays very little attention to those who are already attempting subversion. He misses out the countercultural history of Los Angeles and Southern California, which should include a trajectory stemming from the 1960s hippie/anti-war movement towards contemporary ecological thought, and direct action groups such as Earth First! Perhaps it is within these cultures of resistance that Davis may find hope, or has he 'given up' on those 'Others' campaigning and acting for change? Davis does have a tendency to paint a picture of despair - one that may be unrecognisable not only to those who live in LA but also those in the global city.

Despite these two criticisms, *Ecology of Fear* is a valuable contribution and timely alternative to much of the literature on LA that has been so dominant during the 1990s. As he states, there is a pressing need for a re-examination of the relationship between the social and the environment: it is one that the authorities need to investigate and *invest* in. Davis fully exposes how social problems in LA actually create those environmental disasters: that the two perform a dialectical role in the construction, culture and fabric of the city.

These sporting times

These sporting times

Andrew Blake

Sport's omnipresence helps us to ignore it. The ever present grind of wins and defeats, records set and 'personalities' interrogated is part of the everyday background noise of contemporary culture, and too often critical projects - such as *Soundings* - have left it at that. From newspapers and news broadcasts, we may identify patterns such as the shaping of the year through seasonal sporting contests, and the rise and fall of particular teams or athletes. We may also recognise changes in the representation of sport, welcoming or loathing phenomena such as the privatisation of broadcasting, or the current respectability of football (and/or the concomitant decline of cricket) in the media-national sporting psyche. But for many of us turning that background noise into more harmonious - or indeed discordant - patterns requires special effort.

This is equally so for the committed performer or fan, partially blinded to all beyond their discipline or team, and to the many for whom sport remains the most trivial of pursuits and obsessive interest in it a sign of perpetual immaturity. This first *Soundings* overview of sport includes the views of all the above - the Manchester United fan, the champion amateur kickboxer, and the dispassionate observer of televised sport, all make telling contributions to the collection. And they do so in a way which makes it easier for all of us to perceive those harmonies, and then to think more forcefully about the discords which result when, as Alan Tomlinson makes clear, the rhetorics of sport are denied by the economic and political effects. The themes addressed here, resulting from such ambivalences, involve issues of identity; of legal and political intervention in sport; and of the changing roles of capital in general, and communications technologies in particular, in both facilitating sport and changing its meaning.

Identity: ethnicity, gender, nation

The first theme article of this issue begins with Carol Smith's response to the recent National Portrait Gallery exhibition, *British Sporting Heroes*. She addresses the ways in which, under the influence of the New Labour regime, an exhibition tries to be inclusive, but does not acknowledge the histories which have produced a multicultural Britain. This, she argues, can obscure the continuing gendered and ethnic tensions which remain in sport as in the rest of British society. Likewise, when the England team is led by someone of Asian-Muslim origin, we might think of cricket as a successful example of the British transformation to multiculturalism. Steve Greenfield and Guy Osborn, in discussing the changing place of cricket in the nation, identify some of those continuing ethnic tensions, and the ways in which they were policed from within, and without, the sport during the recent World Cup.

While we often reflect on the changing fan base (such as the Pakistani presence in Britain) as an index of the deconstruction of unitary patriotism, the identity of the sports performer is too often taken for granted. In particular female competitors are still represented from a position of feminised difference. Gemma Bryden describes her first few moments of competition, in which a moment of epiphany, as with so many athletes, centres on the successful absorption of pain. Her positive representation of female aggression makes us think hard about both the gendered nature of sport, and interest in sport. If aggression, and the giving as well as receiving of pain through contest, continue to be written of(f) as implicitly unfortunate traits of masculinity, then it will remain very difficult to persuade more British women to take up sport, and to persuade male-dominated organisations such as the FA (still, spectacularly, institutionally sexist) to take women's sport seriously. The world-wide growth of women's football, celebrated joyously in this year's World Cup - significantly, with a final contested by the USA and China - will therefore pass the UK by, as the changing world men's game did from the 1930s to the 1960s.

Law and politics

My examination of the furore over fox hunting, and the wider problem of field sports, offers a sense of the different national identities available through the very definition of sport, and of the ways in which these ideological and moral disputes are addressed through legal and political structures, many of which - though applied to activities which claim 'traditional' status - are part of the general commodified 'modernisation' of sport. The law as it affects cricket is looked at in more detail by Steve Greenfield and Guy Osborn. Cricket like field sports attaches itself to a mythologised past while perforce confronting the forces of modernisation. Both accounts point up the increasing importance of the law in professional and participant sport alike. Much of the sporting world is now concerned principally with the flow in intangible 'rights'. Adam Brown comments on the now almost constant legal and political intervention in the running of England's most successful football team (i.e. the one with most rights at its disposal), Manchester United; the effort to keep United from competing in the 1999/2000 FA Cup is widely attributed to a government which is pathologically keen to win not the World Cup itself, but the hosting of the Finals; for reasons which Alan Tomlinson's account of sports ceremonial helps to clarify.

Where then must we place New Labour after two years' oversight of sport in Britain? The renaming of the Department for Heritage as Culture, Media and Sport, was a splendid start, and the rhetorical gesture has been followed by some thoughtful uses of lottery money. The Football Task Force, which includes Adam Brown, has been a positive innovation in a sport dominated by unaccountable directors and television moguls, and perhaps sport's finest hour under the current administration was the denial of Rupert Murdoch's attempt to buy Manchester United. But the Task Force also signals the administration's over-concentration on football, which just doesn't need public support in the same way as cricket or athletics, both caught in a spiral of diminishing expectation, achievement, and educational opportunity. In partial acknowledgement of this imbalance, in July 1999 Tony Banks, prime chaser of the World Cup dream, was replaced as Minister for Sport by Kate Hoey: equally forthright, but broader in experience and expertise. Nonetheless her first, unwise, public pronouncement was on the Manchester United question.

As Adam Locks points out, while its pro-football populism is doubtless intended to identify New Labour with the People's Game, in its continuing tendency to privilege style over substance, New Labour is closer to bodybuilding. It produces policy documents rather than policies. Yet the paradigm case in New Labour's relationship with sport is not a pose but a genuine, but troubling, intervention: it is not Tony Banks's broadcast celebration of a winning goal by a Norwegian playing for a northern football team as a 'national' victory that is the issue, but the Party's decision to allow Formula One motor racing a few more years of tobacco sponsorship even when it was known that F1 chief, Bernie Ecclestone, was a major donor to the Labour Party. Formula One is the second most important global sport, and as the rollcall of past and present winning team names (McLaren, Williams, Lotus, BRM) indicates, it is the greatest continuous success story in post-war British sporting endeavour. The sport is tied into a huge global public through broadcasting, and its continuing association with nicotine addiction is therefore particularly unedifying. Equally so was the threat to withdraw various of the more successful teams from Britain, where R&D and engine building are still concentrated. New Labour's concession to its funder's request was politically inept as well as morally wrong, and doubtless led Murdoch to think he still enjoyed a free house in British cultural politics.

Capital and communications

The loss of Formula One coverage by BBC television was an early sign both of the 'national' broadcaster's move away from investment in sport, and of the increasing influence of commercial pressures on the sporting calendar. Whatever happens in the private spaces used by golf clubs or fishing syndicates, the everyday impact of contemporary sports is via the still semi-public space of the broadcast media. Steve Hawes reflects on a particular moment in the televising of football, in which technology and broadcast values combined to present the footballer as personality rather than artisan.

Alan Tomlinson reviews the spectacular, made-for-television ceremonies at the Olympic and World Cup Finals, noting that their neurotic representation of local difference hides the true globalisation presided over by the organising committees, with their Swiss tax-lite regimes of accumulation - in all of which corporatism the ceremonial representation of the events seems rather more important than the actual sporting contests. Alistair Loadman considers a less public aspect of globalisation, the arrival of an Americanised form of wrestling at a small town in Hampshire, and the ways in which this globalised form, learned from television, signals the future of sport as media-dominated entertainment rather than genuine contest with unpredictable outcome. Looking at a related aspect of the broadcast future, Simon Cook forwards from his Paris address an email correspondence with the BBC, who currently appear reluctant to spend any money on sports coverage; they do not have the rights to represent the Premiership as part of their international programming. As Simon implies, this has implications for his identity as 'an Englishman abroad'.

Which takes us back to nation and identity. If (despite the recent appointment of upfront sports fan Greg Dyke as Director General) the BBC continues to move to a position of 'post-sportism', choosing to spend its money on 'news' channels no-one wants to watch, then one of the most important ways in which the nation (by which I mean the UK) has been constructed since the 1950s will disappear. The postmodern, globalised presentation of sport which will replace it is quite simply incapable of carrying that burden of representation. The Corporation and Government alike will have to sanction this change with their eyes open.

An old man, and a new

This will not mean that the pressures placed on athletes themselves will become any lighter. Early in May 1999 it was announced that the body of George Mallory had been discovered at about 26,000 feet on the north face of Mount Everest; he had died there in 1926, and it was unclear whether or not he had reached the summit. Commentators reflected at length on the equipment he had used, a mixture of tweed and heavy woollens of the sort still to be found on the backs of deerstalkers in the Scottish highlands, but nothing like the hi-tech light, waterproof and windcheating gear used by climbers today. This was a displacement of the real argument. For all their gear, one in five of those attempting the summit of Everest during the 1990s have died in the attempt; 'adventure holidays' involving dangerous adrenaline-rush sports are a big growth area; twenty-one people died in July 1999 while 'canyoning' in Switzerland (and needless to say the world's Volvo drivers then clamoured for all such adrenaline sports to be banned). The real target here was the gentlemanly adventurer. Mallory was characterised, without much apparent nostalgia, as a representative of a sporting past.

The death of an amateur, homo-eroticised English gentleman, a composite of Lytton Strachey, Lord Raglan, and Captain Oates, was used to withdraw, finally, social sanction from that cheerfully naive imperial explorer's masculinity which he embodied.

There is so far, however, no acceptable substitute; indeed, far from embracing the obvious alternative, the new lass/laddism of the après-ski world, it seems that we still require our sporting heroes to be Sir Galahad, as Mallory was dubbed by some of his admirers. Two weeks after the Mallory story the *News of the World* announced a sporting victory of its own. The paper had successfully hunted down Laurence Dallaglio, then the current captain of the England rugby union team (the only even vaguely successful English team competing in major professional men's sport). They set-up a seemingly innocent conversation in which he boasted of taking, and dealing in, cocaine. When exposed, Dallaglio admitted to having lied, but to little else beyond a routine young person's nibbling on the forbidden fruit. He thereon lost the captaincy in a rugby World Cup year. Asked why they had chosen the England captain, rather than the hundreds of other normal young (and therefore occasional recreational drug using) sports people whom it could have chosen to 'expose', the paper's editor claimed that it was a matter of public interest to pursue those in positions of responsibility and influence. The successful athlete has always walked the tightrope between champion and scapegoat, and the media's attempts to police this boundary underline the continuing ambivalence of sporting lives and identities - of sporting heroes, British and otherwise - in the contemporary world.

This sporting nation

Carol Smith

Though a step in the right direction, Carol Smith
*argues that 'British Sporting Heroes' still exhibits
too narrow a representation of Britishness.*

The ministry and the museum

> In the 80's I failed to get them [the National Portrait Gallery] to accept a
> portrait of Tony Benn by Topolski then in the 90s they turned down a portrait
> bust of Eric Cantona. Times have changed now I am a Minister.[1]

The exhibition 'British Sporting Heroes' at the National Portrait Gallery
(October 1998 - January 1999), which was suggested by then Minister for Sport
Tony Banks, did indeed signal that times had changed with a Labour
government. The populist and inclusive national subject matter was a radical
and welcome departure for an institution better known for its Royal portraits.
It also marked the apotheosis of the Blairite appropriation of sport as the sign
of New Labour/New Britain which had begun at the 1996 Labour Party
Conference. Here the lyric of the Baddiel and Skinner/Lightning Seeds' Euro
96 anthem - perhaps significantly, a song by England supporters - had been
adapted to 'Labour's coming home'. What follows examines the exhibition as a
test case of change; an analysis of the representations of Britishness new, radical
or otherwise offered under New Labour.

   That the exhibition marked a significant shift in policy on the part of a

---

1. Tony Banks quoted in the London *Evening Standard*, 16.10.98.

national institution is indicated by the public statements of Tony Banks and Charles Saumarez Smith, the National Portrait Gallery's (NPG's) Director. Both stressed that the aim of the exhibition was to open up and democratise the Gallery, Saumarez Smith writing that '... we would like to think that by holding an exhibition on a subject of such universal appeal we may encourage a new audience into the gallery', while Banks was quoted in the press as stating: 'I hope the exhibition will encourage many people to come to the gallery who would not normally dare cross the threshold.'[2] Saumarez Smith's rather abstract 'universal appeal' contrasts somewhat with Tony Banks' specific appeal to 'people'. Still, both imply that the exhibition was designed ideologically both to define the British people through their sporting heroes, and to make them connoisseurs of the arts, thereby establishing the sense of connection among the fields of endeavour served by the new Ministry for Culture, Heritage and Sport: a populism which will be reinforced by a forthcoming NPG exhibition of pop heroes.

British sporting heroes

The exhibition was hung in a linear, chronological progression covering the majority of competitive sports (field sports were not included). As the press release stated, the individual images were chosen to produce a narrative of sport as 'a phenomenon that has evolved and changed with our national history and economic development, from the days of the paid champion to the independently super-rich contemporary star'.[3] The inter-relationship between British national history and the history of sport in Britain, here made explicit, via the notion of evolution, as a natural connection, was a basic assumption behind the exhibition. The recurrent notion that to represent all sports is to represent all British peoples is exemplified by the cover of the catalogue.

The cover illustration, extending from front to back, is a composite of the facial segments of eight portraits which can be read as representative of the

---

2. Charles Saumarez Smith, *The Book of British Sporting Heroes*, compiled by J. Huntington-Whitely, National Portrait Gallery Publications, London, 1998, p7; Tony Banks quoted in *Evening Standard*, 16.10.98.
3. ' British Sporting Heroes', Press Notice, National Portrait Gallery, London, October 1998.

types of sports, sporting heroes and therefore kinds of British identity celebrated by the exhibition. Thus across the cover from left to right are images of: James Robinson, 1850 (horse racing); Wavell Wakefield, 1923 (rugby union); Jack Hobbs, 1920 (cricket); Naseem Hamed, 1996 (boxing); W.G. Grace, 1890 (cricket); David, Lord Burghley 1926 (athletics); Kitty Godfreed, 1924 (tennis); George Best, 1968 (football). It is obvious from this list that it has been designed not only to take in a variety of sports through a period of time but also to encapsulate the different facets of class, gender, race and ethnicity that reflect the historical and contemporary definition of 'British'. The catalogue's essay, by historian Richard Holt, addressing the changing dynamics of sporting and national identities, furthers the exhibition's claims of an inclusive representation of British sporting heroes.

In comparison, the last sport and nationality-themed exhibition mounted in the National Portrait Gallery, *The Sporting Thirties* (February - May 1985), neither acknowledged the dimension of identity and difference, nor made any explicit attempt at being inclusive of British society in terms of gender, ethnicity, nationality or class. It organised the exhibits by sport, and its catalogue offered minimal information, consisting of a folded A3 sheet with only the barest details and a couple of black and white images. (This exhibition was, of course, held under a Thatcher Conservative government; while Thatcher's minimalist notion of society and contempt for sport is well known, it should also be said that the arts establishment was never fully complicit with Thatcherism).

The minister and the people

Undoubtedly there has been change for the better. However, as publications such as *The Moderniser's Dilemma* and *Soundings 10* have suggested, the rush to celebrate this exhibition or any other product of the Blair government in terms of its modernisation of traditional Conservative values needs to be checked.[4] Andrew Blake has shown that such a valorisation, especially in terms of heritage culture, needs to be aware of the consequences of the

---

4. A. Coddington & M. Perryman (eds) *The Moderniser's Dilemma, Radical Politics in the Age of Blair*, Lawrence & Wishart, London 1998; Alan Finlayson, 'Tony Blair and the Jargon of Modernisation', *Soundings*, 10, Lawrence and Wishart, London 1998; and see the group of essays in that collection exploring the anniversary of the Empire Windrush.

process of modernisation New Labour employs. Blake describes the Blairite process of modernisation as one of conservation rather than the wholesale revolution imagined by old Labour and defines it thus: What new Labour is trying to achieve through this shift [modernisation] is retrolution: disguising the future as the past to present it as palatable.[5] The 'British Sporting Heroes' exhibition would seem to be a prime example of retrolution, offering a re-interpretation of British culture and identity through the overarching narrative of sport. However, the past which it employs to present a palatable multicultural British present arguably undermines the democratising and inclusive intentions of the exhibition.

This tension can be exemplified by the photographs of Tony Banks at the opening of the exhibition which appeared in all the national broad-sheets and much of the regional press, part of a wide coverage which made this one of the most heavily-reviewed exhibitions ever mounted by the gallery. Banks is shown, in belted raincoat and Chelsea FC scarf, standing in front of a large photograph, 'Crowd at a Football Tie, Norwich, 1939', which was positioned at the entrance of the exhibition. Clearly visible behind him, the crowd in the original photograph is also standing, in overcoats and hats - mostly flat caps - and is predominantly male (there are two women) and totally white. The effect, surely intentional, is to make it look as if Banks is himself standing in the crowd. Here is the Minister for Sport along with the people who watch sport, welcoming them into an exhibition of their heroes. The football crowd of the past is therefore shown to have already contained the future - the Minister's idea of the future. While there are signs of change - Banks is the only member of the crowd whose scarf is obviously a team scarf - these do not disturb a potential identification of the contemporary visitor to the exhibition with the crowd. As long, that is, as this visitor is male and white. All the pictorial and rhetorical strategies of inclusion noted above are reliant on the continued predominant presentation of the future - the crowd, the nation - as male and white. Of course this might be a *new* male whiteness which embraces a multicultural nationality, but even this multiculturalism is, it becomes clear, shown within a very clearly delimited, retrolutionary view of post-Imperial Britain.

---

5. A. Blake, 'Retrolution: Culture and Heritage in a Young Country', in *The Moderniser's Dilemma*, p144.

Portraying empire

The National Portrait Gallery was founded in 1856 with the first meeting of the Trustees on 9 February 1857 where the Resolutions, which governed acquisitions, were agreed. The central historical mission is encapsulated in Rule 1:

> The rule which the Trustees desire to lay down to themselves, in either making purchases or receiving presents, is to look to the celebrity of the person represented rather then to the merit of the artist. They will attempt to estimate that celebrity without any bias to political or religious party. Nor will they consider great faults and errors, even though admitted on all sides, as any sufficient ground for excluding any portrait, which may be valuable in illustrating the civil, ecclesiastical, or literary history of the country.[6]

Anyone who walks through the three floors of the NPG's permanent displays, arranged in historical sequence from the Tudors on the top floor to the early twentieth century on the bottom, is left in no doubt who or what makes up the 'civil, ecclesiastical, or literary history of the country'- white, English males. The small number of women are there mostly through familial connections (e.g. Royalty) or as tokenised, exemplary symbols of the feminine contribution to history (e.g. Florence Nightingale). The even fewer portraits featuring non-whites are concentrated in the Victorian rooms. In them, non-whites are never the sole named sitters but are always represented in relation to the main (hence 'British') white focus. One title, 'Clive receiving the Homage of Mir Jaffier after the Battle of Plessey' gives the general rule. Just as no connection is made between the heroes of industrialisation and the institution of slavery, so in the next room High Victorian culture is presented in isolation from the subjugation of non-Western peoples.

That such a collection is only now being modernised for the millennium is a remarkable testament to the long influence of Victorian attitudes to history and Empire. As if to testify to the problematic hegemony of this white British history and identity which the permanent collection offers, the gallery has mounted several temporary exhibitions which have emphasised the historical connections of Empire and cultural representation, and of the impact both of black slaves and of living Britons of African descent. October

---

6. Quoted in *The National Portrait Gallery*, Charles Saumarez Smith.

1990 to March 1991, for instance, saw 'The Raj, India and the British Empire', a major exhibition which went well beyond the gallery's core business of portraiture, memorably re-examining India as represented through Anglo-Indian landscape art. More recently and more typically of the gallery's work, 'Ignatius Sancho: An African Man of Letters' (January - May 1997) contextualised Sancho within the culture of eighteenth-century Britain, offering a corrective to the symbolic or decorative images of blackness in portraits such as 'Louise De Keroualle, Duchess of Portsmouth' in the main collection. 'black Power' (February - June 1998) was a collection of twenty-four portraits of contemporary black Britons by Donald MacLellan.

While such exhibitions are to be welcomed, their isolation from the permanent displays arguably prevents them from challenging the NPG's Imperial inheritance, especially since the layout of the gallery allows visitors to visit either the permanent collection or the temporary exhibitions. Still, these exhibitions and the millennium modernisation testify to the Gallery's importance as a prime site for recognising how British history and identity has been less white than *white-centred*, with non-whites functioning transactionally in the service of constructing a homogeneous white Britishness. It offers, quite literally, an institutional view of how 'blackness' and black experience has been inscribed/written/painted strategically off centre, on the margins of British identity, and latterly how 'our' national institutions have attempted to contest or correct the default positioning of whiteness.

Qualifying historically

So the gallery as much as any other contemporary institution can be seen to be working through a process of positive change, and 'British Sporting Heroes', with its popular renegotiation of the national, is as much influenced by the gallery's own history as by the modernising impetus of New Labour. Certainly, the exhibition's 250 images did seem to have been chosen to reflect the contribution of multi-ethnic, national and gendered British people, as already suggested in the discussion of the cover of the catalogue. Hence of the 250 artefacts there were representations of 220 men and 30 women; 235 white British, 15 non-white; of those whose nationality was specified there were 28 Scots, 21 Welsh, 9 Irish and 2 others (the Italian jockey Frankie Dettori, and K.S. Ranjitsinhji, cricketer and Indian prince, whose complex identities are discussed below).

What the bare numbers do not show, and the alphabetical organisation of the catalogue obscures, is the historical positioning of the non-white, non-male portraits. With a few exceptions the black portraits are from the 1950s to the present day, paralleling the post-war immigration of black Britons to Britain. So while it might seem as if this exhibition is repeating the marginalisation of non-whites and women in the permanent displays, actually what it does is to mark historically when they began to be included in mainstream sports. Holt's catalogue essay echoes the chronological hanging's linear, progressive narratives of inclusion. He differentiates a long line of white male heroes by class and economics; the early pugilists and pedestrians who were paid by aristocrats; the gentlemen amateurs; the modern professionals; and lastly the contemporary superstars. This overarching narrative is augmented by the presence of women in the early twentieth century, and by the rise of the black British sports hero in the contemporary period. The captions and text in the catalogue follow this progressive line of inclusion in pointing out, for example, the first appearance of a black sports person in an international, as with Billy Boston (rugby league) for the 1954 Great Britain touring side to Australia.

> 'Unsurprisingly, there is a tension between this attempt to represent modern Britishness and its previous constructions'

However there is an unresolved tension between the way in which Holt foregrounds the arguably contesting narrative notions of gender, ethnicity, class and nationality, and the overarching historical and alphabetical ordering of the catalogue. As much as this exhibition can be read as democratising and modernising both the gallery and our conception of the British Sporting Hero, it never thoroughly examines its own relationship to the concept of history as progressive inclusion, a concept deeply embedded in certain aspects of the historiography of the period of imperialism itself.

Representing empire - the slave and the prince

That there continues to be such a tension between this attempt to represent modern Britishness and its previous constructions is not surprising, since of course the employment of sport in the establishment of British identity and its problematics have long been recognised. In this sense it would be a mistake to expect one Victorian institution (competitive sport) to radically critique another (the National Portrait Gallery), especially through the art form of portraiture, whose history is largely one of patronage by rich individuals. Holt attempts to elide this tension by aligning the aristocratic past of sport and gambling with the contemporary agents, sponsorship and advertising - isolating the period in between as a heroic past when 'Sport defined much of what the British admired about themselves and what others admired about them, before the world's media began the process of narrowing national differences'.[7] The circularity of this description raises a similar difficulty to the photograph of Banks 'in' the crowd. The representation of the late Victorian era and early twentieth century as an unproblematic and heroic period for sport (before the intervention of the media) is a common one, and dangerously nostalgic. As long as who the 'others' are is not specified, or how exactly 'they' were watching or playing sport is not particularised, the mutual appreciation society of Britain and the world is preserved. Introduce the pre-Victorian history of slavery or the narrative of colonial expansion though a specific sport such as cricket, especially in relationship to India, and a less comforting, or at least less straightforward narrative, ensues. Of course, in the visual arts, especially portraiture, it is hard to ignore the presence of racial 'others' as they are usually marked by skin colour. So to include such images in this narrative of British inclusion, strategies of displacement and containment have to be invoked.

One such example is of pugilist Tom Cribb, whose portrait is an ink and watercolour scene of his fight in 1811 against Tom Molyneux. The portrait shows a ring in the open air surrounded by a rowdy, cheering crowd of white males and females in the foreground and carriages in the middle ground, clearly spatially demarcating contemporary class differences. Cribb is shown, flanked by the corner men and referee, delivering the blow which broke Molyneux's jaw in the ninth round. In the watercolour, Molyneux's blackness is obvious from the hue of his skin, while the catalogue marks his racial identity obliquely, describing him as 'the American Tom Molyneux, an ex-slave who made a name for himself in England', 'ex-slave' signifying black. Staffordshire pottery figures of the two men, with equally 'obvious' ethnic

7. R. Holt, 'Champions, Heroes and Celebrities: Sporting Greatness and the British Public' in *The Book of British Sporting Heroes*, p24.

colouring, also appear as illustrations (without comment) in Holt's catalogue essay. That Molyneux is carefully defined *by the catalogue* as 'American' and an 'ex-slave' and Cribb as an English national hero denudes the portrait of a larger frame - that of British involvement in the slave trade. The portrait is inscribed as a battle of nationalities, the American side represented by an ex-slave because 'they' had slaves. A very different narrative, which might link the two fighters in their exploitation by the aristocracy and merchants of Britain, is also possible, though this would fracture the hegemonic difference of the British invoked by Holt and others.

A contrasting but equally complex example is the portrait of K.S. Ranjitsinhji, otherwise known as Colonel His Highness Shri Sir Ranjitsinhji Vibhaji, Maharaj Jam Sahib of Nawangar (or 'Smith' while at Cambridge, and 'Ranji' while batting for Sussex and England). The portrait is a photograph of Ranjitsinhji at the crease, bat ready to strike a yet unseen ball. As with the representation of Molyneux, the portrait makes visible his non-white racial identity. The catalogue entry also specifies nationality, but one whose potential disruption is subsumed within narratives of class and sporting prowess:

> The Rajput prince was first selected to play for England in 1896, and rising above the inevitable opposition to having an Indian in the team he scored 62 and 154 not out in his first two innings [against Australia].

As his full name with its combination of Indian and British titles suggests, Ranjitsinhji was a member of an elite group of Anglophiles whose class, education and wealth aligned him with the English aristocracy. None of this is discussed in the catalogue. Instead it is his sporting skill which naturalises him, a convenient side-stepping of the complex dynamics of class, the coloniser and the colonised. What mention is made of Empire merely guarantees that Ranjitsinhji would have passed any cricket test set by Norman Tebbit, since he voluntarily subscribes not only to playing for England but to imperialism itself:

> A great Imperialist himself, Ranji's *Jubilee Book of Cricket* was fulsomely dedicated to Queen Victoria and in it he wrote that cricket was 'certainly amongst the most powerful links which keep our Empire together … one of the great contributions the British people have made to the cause of humanity'.

Here the British imperial past is rendered in terms of one of the constituents volunteering its inclusion, even praising it, through the narrative of sport. This is indeed retrolution - Victorian England is represented as always already, peacefully and by choice, multicultural, just as should be contemporary Britain. In Blake's terms the future can then be presented as the past because the past has been represented as already inclusively British. Of course this, as with the Cribb example, relies on a very limited and restrictive interpretation of British history, Empire and sport, certainly not one which is marked by the contestory work of such critics as C.L.R. James and Stuart Hall.

Of course there's black in the Union Jack

This narrative of elective assimilation does prepare the viewer for the increased number of black sporting heroes from the 1950s on, though this kind of preparation is one which obviates explanation of their historical context. Holt's essay marks the 1980s as the point of the emergence of the black British sporting hero with no mention of any post-war pattern of migration and settlement from the former British colonies.

This narrative of silent assimilation of the contemporary black portraits is further effected by the oblique racial and ethnic descriptions of the black heroes in the catalogue. Of the fifteen non-white portraits only seven captions mention race or ethnicity, and this is often done obliquely through the mention of family origins or because they were the first black person to play for Britain. Ethnicity is particularised through familial relationships in the following cases: Naseem Hamed (boxing) has a 'Yemeni father'; Randolph Turpin (boxing) has an elder brother until whose appearance 'black boxers had been excluded from contesting a British title'; Rory Underwood (rugby union) has an 'enthusiastic Malaysian mother'; Fatima Whitbread (javelin) is of 'Cypriot parentage'. Billy Boston and Ellery Hanley (rugby league) are the first black players to play for and captain Great Britain respectively. There is no mention of ethnicity in the other eight cases.

Arguably this silent assimilation might signal the successful transformation of the white-centred Victorian British identity proffered by the NPG's permanent collection, such that there is no need to particularise the racial or ethnic identity of the individual British sporting hero. An examination of the press reviews of the exhibition could be said to affirm this view. Only one review mentioned racial and ethnic difference in the make up of Britishness and found the exhibition wanting in this respect. 'British in this context is very close to its usual meaning - white, English and male.'[8] Most debated the choice of heroes and bemoaned the loss of a Britain of yesteryear conjured up by portraits from the 1930s, especially those of athletes Harold Abrahams, Eric Liddell and David, Lord Burghley - all made famous by the film 'Chariots of Fire'.

Perhaps; but this assumption of inclusion without any particularisation of the differing histories of access to, and success in, sport of the different racial groups in Britain builds a falsely positive homogeneity of British identity. It denies the positive communal changes that different immigrant populations have effected for themselves and on the nation as a whole. Important as individual sports people are in their own right, the literal and symbolic effect of grouping them and providing them with their differing histories would counter the Victorian model of elective assimilation described above.

And we must remember that in the larger social context of contemporary Britain outside of sport, the Macpherson Report into the murder of Stephen Lawrence, and the mid-1999 nail bombings of what some still see as marginal racial and sexual communities, would suggest that such hope for an assumed complete transformation of mainstream white society is premature. The Macpherson Report's conclusions on institutional racism provide official acknowledgement of structural racism, without being able to hold any individuals responsible. This sense that racism is simultaneously everywhere and nowhere implies that a popular confidence in achieved, assimilated multiculturalism is premature to say the least. The 'British Sporting Heroes' exhibition exists as much in this context as it does in the longer history of imperialism; the challenges both contexts bring to assumed notions of Britishness need to be articulated as well as visually included. As important as it is to *see* these non-white faces, their contesting voices and histories need as obvious attention and inscription.

Coloured white heroes

However in one limited sense the Union Jack has indeed become full of 'colour'. Richard Dyer and others have recently described the visual discourses

---

8. *West End Extra*, London, 20.11.98.

in which whiteness has culturally been associated with Christianity, progress and colonial hero(ine)ism. An analysis of the exhibition's non-contemporary portraits of female sporting heroes through Dyer's focus on white femininity as the pre-eminent positive guarantee of the rightness of colonial enterprises would be a useful extension of the studies of both sport and nationality.

A final analysis of two contemporary portraits might suggest a way forward. Olympic hurdler Sally Gunnell is shown in a highly posed and stylised colour photograph. She appears in an almost balletic pose, clothed in a leotard-like running costume, torso extended over outstretched legs against a brilliant blue background, eyes closed. While it is obvious that Gunnell is white, she is as obviously heavily tanned. Dyer is not the first to suggest that tanning is associated with healthiness and fitness; it has been a commonplace since Coco Chanel in the 1930s. Dyer's reading of it as a way by which white people might inhabit what have been culturally characterised as black traits is especially pertinent for sports, specifically recent athletics with its predominance of black champions. Inhabit but not become:

> A tanned person is just that - a white person who has acquired a darker skin. There is no loss of prestige in this. On the contrary, not only does he or she retain the signs of whiteness ... not only does tanning bespeak a wealth and life style largely at white people's disposition, but it also displays white people's right to be various, literally to incorporate into themselves features of other peoples.[9]

That this process has become so normalised, especially within the arena of sport, partly explains the lack of comment on it hitherto. It is only when the process of inhabiting 'a darker skin' is surreally represented as in the portrait of rugby union forward Fran Cotton that the seemingly neutral aesthetic presentation of Gunnell is politicised in Dyer's terms.

The Cotton portrait is also a photograph, a black and white action shot from a 1977 British Lions match against New Zealand. Cotton is flanked by two other Lions waiting for a throw from a line out. All are totally covered in mud. This portrait elicited two very different readings in the press, all the more

---

9. R. Dyer, *White*, Routledge, London, p49.

startling given that most reviews failed to isolate any specific portraits. Chris Smith of *The Daily Telegraph* described it as 'the shot in which a caked Fran Cotton rises ominously from the mud as if in some terrible throwback to the Somme'. Compare Brian Sewell's description in the *Evening Standard* of 'Fran Cotton, rugby forward, represented as a cross-eyed warthog with a Rastafarian hair-do, slopped in mud'.[10]

The extreme symbolism of these two readings can be read as displacements of Cotton's 'blackness'. Smith invokes 'Englishness' in dramatic terms - the tragedy of the trenches of World War One - to stabilise for the viewer Cotton's heroic, white status. Sewell relies on ironic racism with his animalistic Rastafarian, signalling through a knowing deployment of 'humour' to undercut any destabilising or permanent colouring of Cotton. While in the case of Gunnell there is a normalised and arguably feminised acceptance of colouring, the Cotton portrait seems to mark the limit of such a process. Britishness can be black, it seems, only if it remains bounded in the black male body, or as a fashionable addition to white femininity. Whiteness and Britishness remain indivisible, blackness still an excess to be welcomed for its sporting prowess.

The 'British Sporting Heroes' exhibition does mark a change, offering potentially positive challenges to 'our' sporting nation in the ways it can be read to represent and contest a pluralistic construction of Britishness and sport. But it is only a limited beginning. We need to continue to represent, legislate and participate to win.

10. G. Smith, 'Sporting heroes making exhibitions of themselves', *The Daily Telegraph*, London, 17.10.98; B. Sewell, 'Hail to the conquering icons', the London, *Evening Standard*, 5.11.98.

Where's my match?

A British subject interrogates the national broadcaster

Simon Cook

The game is up for Simon Cook *as the BBC reject his pleas for broadcasting football to Europe.*

Being an Englishman abroad, I had cable TV installed. The BBC have a channel named BBC Prime which is basically BBC1. However this channel does not show Match of Day (the lads, and even some women I know, can relate to Saturday night 10:40, Gary Lineker, Alan Hansen and Trevor Brooking). So I sent the BBC an e-mail asking why and here are copies of the correspondences.

```
From:     Simon Cook [SMTP:spcook@....com]
Sent:     02 June 1999 18:55
To:       worldwidetv.letters@bbc.co.uk
Subject:  Match of the Day

Will BBC Prime show Match of the Day when the new
English football season starts?
```

From: Worldwidetv
Letters <worldwidetv.letters@bbc.co.uk>

To: "'Simon Cook'" <spcook@....com>
Subject: RE: Match of the Day
Date: Thu, 3 Jun 1999 11:01:17 +0100

Dear Mr Simon Cook
Thank you for your email.
I regret to say that BBC Prime have no plans to transmit 'Match of the Day'.

Best regards
Mario Giannini
Customer Relations Department
BBC World & BBC Prime

From: Simon Cook [SMTP:spcook@....com]
Sent: 03 June 1999 11:29
To: worldwidetv.letters@bbc.co.uk
Subject: RE: Match of the Day

Is there a reason why?

From: Worldwidetv
Letters <worldwidetv.letters@bbc.co.uk>
To: "'Simon Cook'" <spcook@....com>
Subject: RE: Match of the Day
Date: Thu, 3 Jun 1999 12:15:17 +0100

Dear Simon Cook
Further to your query about 'Match of the Day', you may be aware that it has become increasingly difficult, because of the complexity of rights, to broadcast sport. Rights to transmit sport on the terrestrial channels BBC1 and BBC2 do not

include rights for the satellite channels. The cost of acquiring international broadcast rights has become prohibitive in the face of competition from satellite channels dedicated to sport and in addition to this we would not be able to screen the tournaments that the viewers would want to see - such as The World Cup Cricket, FA Cup Final or Wimbledon etc. The rights are only sold on a country by country basis as the events organisers are able to make a great deal more money this way. This includes programmes like 'Grandstand' or 'Match of the Day', where the rights to transmit coverage of events shown on these programmes are sold by the individual event organisers.

It was decided, therefore, that BBC PRIME and BBC WORLD would exclude sport and concentrate on entertainment, news and information respectively. BBC WORLD does have two minute sports bulletins after the main hourly news bulletins and this includes news of all major sporting events occurring around the world.

In addition to this, as a special service to those interested in the World Cup Cricket, from Friday 14 May at 1857 GMT BBC WORLD has been transmitting details of the latest scores, batting and bowling performances and other facts from the 1999 Cricket World Cup in a series of one minute scoreboards.

They will be transmitted daily at 0157 GMT, 1457 GMT, 1557 GMT and 1857 GMT until Sunday 20 June. I hope that the above goes some way towards explaining the reasons behind the absence of sport

on *BBC PRIME* and *BBC WORLD* and *I hope you will
continue to enjoy watching our channels.*

*Once again, thank you for taking the trouble to
write to us and please do not hesitate to contact
us again if you have any further queries.*

Best regards

*Mario Giannini
Customer Relations Department
BBC World & BBC Prime*

From: Simon Cook [SMTP:spcook@....com]
Sent: 03 June 1999 13:20
To: worldwidetv.letters@bbc.co.uk
Subject: Match of the Day

Thank you very much for your full and comprehensive
answer. To put it simply, are you trying to tell
me that you've been fucked-over by the likes of
Sky TV?

*From: Worldwidetv
Letters <worldwidetv.letters@bbc.co.uk>
To: "'Simon Cook'" <spcook@....com>
Subject: RE: Match of the Day
Date: Thu, 3 Jun 1999 13:27:50 +0100*

*Dear Mr Cook
Unfortunately I cannot comment on your last email
however as explained before, in light of
competition from satellite/cable broadcasters who
transmit channels dedicated to sport we, as a*

small commercial broadcaster, are unable to bid for the rights to show sporting events. I am sorry that you are disappointed that we do not show sport however I would advise you to enquire as to the possibility of receiving sports channels in your local area.

Best regards

Mario Giannini
Customer Relations Department
BBC World & BBC Prime

Tilting at windmills

Manchester United and the defeat of the BSkyB bid

Adam Brown

United fan Adam Brown *argues that the defeat of Sky was the most significant victory of his team's record-breaking season*

For some of us who've spent the close season celebrating football history being made in the shape of Manchester United's treble of Premier League, FA Cup and European Cup, there has been another victory to add to the list, and it's one in which all football fans should be able to share. On 9 April 1999 Trade Secretary Stephen Byers accepted a Monopolies and Mergers Commission report which declared a proposed takeover of Manchester United by Rupert Murdoch's BSkyB satellite TV company as both anti-competitive and against the public interest. Coupled with the recent ruling in the Restrictive Practices Court (RPC) that the collective and exclusive sale of TV rights is in the public interest, the quasi-judicial institutions of government now appear to be the football fans' best friends. Despite public perception to the contrary, the decision to block the BSkyB bid was arguably the more fundamental of these judgements. If the deal had been allowed to proceed, not only would Europe's biggest club have lost an independence which it has held, and prospered under, for over a hundred years, but the dominant forces in the English game would have become in effect a subsidiary of the global TV empires. Whatever the RPC concluded, that development - of TV owning sports content instead of buying the rights to it - would have been irreversible.

The defeat of BSkyB represented many things, however - not only a line in the sand to the power and influence of television in football. In particular, it was the result of a remarkable campaign led and orchestrated by football fans, most notably the Independent Manchester United Supporters Association (IMUSA) and its sister organisation Shareholders United Against Murdoch (SUAM, now Shareholders United). From the first rumours of the takeover, IMUSA led the campaign to stop it.

The pitch

When a journalist rings you sometime around 6am on a Sunday morning saying that Rupert Murdoch is about to buy your football club, dismay is soon followed by an honest and realistic recognition that there's probably not much that can be done. One of the richest and most powerful people in the world, master of almost all televised British sport, bullier of governments and a man who tends to get his own way, Murdoch needs few introductions. To football fans he has presided over a pay TV-driven revolution in English football, removing the national game from live coverage on terrestrial television, and inaugurating a massive increase in match prices and a gulf in wealth between rich and poor in the game. But IMUSA were ready for a fight. In a dark, smoky, upstairs room of Stretford Trades and Labour Club on 8 September 1998 the officers and close aides of IMUSA gathered to plan what to do. The £623m takeover bid was confirmed as genuine, and had been accepted by United's board. In the now legendary words of one present at the IMUSA meeting, 'Murdoch may have walked all over the world, but he won't walk all over Manchester'.

For their part, commentators lined up to gasp at the audacity of the bid and to rule out any hope fans had of stopping the takeover. 'This is the logical conclusion of football selling its soul to the highest bidder', argued one. 'Who's going to stop him? What chance the simple fans?' crowed Jeff Powell in the *Mail*. Even allies, however sympathetic, were telling United fans that the campaign to stop the takeover was 'tilting at windmills'.

However, for those involved with IMUSA, there was little choice but to fight. The club, already a plc and therefore subject to the whims of the Stock

Exchange and its institutional investors, was to be removed beyond the reach of any fan, a mere cog in the massive Murdoch machine, where its future would ultimately be determined by the over-riding concerns of that machine. For fans who had spent the previous ten years complaining about the Premiership breakaway, price increases, the shifting of fixtures to suit Sky's priorities and a pursuit of profit over any footballing principle, this was a step too far.

To some, Murdoch's purchase of Europe's richest club was the logical extension of an increasing integration of television and football. Although no media corporation has owned a UK football club, such relationships are not new: Italian giants AC Milan are owned by Silvio Berlusconi (of Media Set and Forza Italia infamy) and Paris St Germain are owned by French channel Canal+. Murdoch's Fox TV also owns the LA Dodgers baseball team, among others. So what was the problem here?

For even the most blinkered Manchester United fan, there were grave concerns. The bid was too low; there was no promise of extra cash to buy players; there was the fact that BSkyB would have to recoup the loan secured to buy the club fairly rapidly, some estimating the need for a £50 million a year return from a club which currently makes an annual profit of around £20 million; and that Murdoch has a dire reputation for meddling in companies he buys.

But for IMUSA, there were wider issues. To break the mould and let a TV company wholly own a football club (Sky wanted to buy 100 per cent of shares, making the club a BSkyB subsidiary, removed from the Stock Exchange) would have crossed a Rubicon. The club would be subject to the interests of the parent company, and if that meant selling players, changing leagues or ground location, or playing five Far Eastern tours a year, then that's what would be done. What is more, the deal would have precipitated a range of similar bids for other clubs, landing the future of football wholly in the hands of television. The game would no longer even have the option of determining its own future, protecting the interests of fans and players, resisting the formation of money-driven European Super Leagues. However inept football may be at the moment in resisting the lure of the lucre, it still has the option of rescuing itself. With TV as owners rather than partners, football would only go in one direction - huge amounts of money for the clubs who can muster large TV audiences (already the richest) would be a further nail in the coffin for smaller clubs. This was the overwhelming threat: that the dominant club in English football would be owned by the dominant media corporation, creating a power bloc to the detriment of the poorer, especially lower division, clubs. If a handful of the big clubs were to follow United into media ownership, the self-sustaining wealth gap which the Premier League has already instigated would widen still further. There was little chance of clubs such as Chester, Hull City and Brighton surviving in a world where TV money was hoarded by the few.

Thus, the opposition formed around two concerns: the 'public interest' of the future of the country's most popular sport; and issues of competition within the football 'industry'. The former concern, of public interest, reflects the important place which football occupies in terms of a club's relationship with the local community (and the converse, the community as stakeholder in the club) as well as a more general importance in the nation's cultural, sporting and social life. The latter was a concern with how to sustain meaningful competition both within football - on which the game thrives - and within the pay TV sport market. If United were owned by the monopoly supplier of live TV football, then what chance did any other broadcaster have in the market? This was the concern of the Independent Television Commission, BBC and other pay TV operators who joined the ranks of those opposed to Murdoch.

There were also significant parallels with issues elsewhere. Manchester United plc was owned by the board (17 per cent), institutional shareholders (60 per cent) and around 25,000 individuals (23 per cent). Thatcherism may have come late to football, with most flotations taking place in the early to mid-1990s. However, as with the flotation of the utilities, the fallacy of the notion of share-owning democracy was again exposed. Given Sky's wish to wholly own the club, the individual shareholders would be forced *by law* to sell their stake in a company in which they had an emotional as well as a financial involvement. The inability of individuals to influence let alone over-rule the commercial priorities of the board and institutional share-holders was exposed at the plc annual general meeting in November 1998, when, despite overwhelming opposition from the floor, the board were able to proceed untouched.

An early goal

IMUSA's campaign against the bid involved a number of elements. One was the public relations battle, and in this they had a valuable ally in Rupert Murdoch himself. Already a pariah to many, his power and influence had been of concern way beyond the confines of the football world and there was a well of sympathy - not least from his press rivals - on which to draw. However, it soon became apparent that if the deal was to be blocked it would be government, or its agents, which would have to be persuaded of the damage the takeover would do to United and to football as a whole. This meant, first, getting the Office of Fair Trading, through the then Secretary of State for Trade and Industry, Peter Mandelson, to refer the bid to the Monopolies and Mergers Commission (MMC). That this first victory was achieved by the end of October 1998 was a massive boost for campaigners and the result of tireless work that had seen the DTI and OFT bombarded with submissions, faxes, emails and phone calls. In all the OFT received between 350 and 400 submissions against the takeover, a massive number for such an investigation, and one which resulted in the DTI's fax machine throwing in the towel as the date for referral approached.

The breadth of opposition was huge. This was reflected in the fact that the campaigners received massive support from fans of other clubs in the UK and other countries. From the first week IMUSA were receiving messages of support from some surprising places. This from a Liverpool supporter: 'All genuine Liverpool fans hate Murdoch after the disgusting *Sun* reports of the Hillsborough disaster (and we thank you for the support shown by the Man U fans)'. Despite the common cause, to overcome one of the fiercest rivalries in football was quite something. And this from across the city: 'As a City fan, I'm quite enjoying the turmoil United is in at the moment. On a more serious note, though, and leaving aside such rivalries to think about the good of the game as a whole, I, too, am horrified by recent events.' Support also came from abroad, and valuable links were made between fans' organisations such as L'Elephant Blau at Barcelona, and 'NR12' at Bayern Munich, who even brought in solidarity a huge 'STOP MURDOCH' banner to Bayern's Champions' League match at Old Trafford.

In the final push to get the case referred to the OFT, fans from over twenty English clubs converged on the House of Commons to press the point home to MPs and members of the All Party Football Group, who had been stalwart opponents of the takeover. These fans represented clubs as diverse as Slough Town, Luton and Leeds, all recognising that a further widening of the wealth gap in football and a further domination of the game by TV was as against their interests as it was against those of United fans.

A crucial second

The second round was with the MMC itself. Comprising an economics professor, an industrialist, an environmentalist, a trade unionist and an accountant, the panel held evidence sessions with a massive variety of organisations and individuals. In a list that is reminiscent of a Christmas carol - and a famously repetitive festive terrace song in honour of one Eric Cantona - by the end of the whole shooting match the MMC had seen the following: twelve broadcast companies; seven football authorities; six Premier League clubs; six fans' organisations; five local authorities; three Nationwide League clubs; three trade unions (including the PFA and NUJ); seven other groups (including shareholders and academics); three MPs; as well as Manchester United and BSkyB. They had also received testimony from over three hundred individuals, every single one of whom was against the merger. Indeed, of all those who made submissions to, and appeared before, the MMC, the only ones to support the merger were the six Premier League clubs (all of whom, it was rumoured, were likely to follow United into media ownership) plus Manchester United and BSkyB. Whilst a handful of submissions were somewhat equivocal, believing that commercial restrictions, Chinese walls, or behavioural restrictions could work, the overwhelming majority of the testimonies were whole-heartedly against the merger.

However, what was curious was that in a field of public protest more usually associated with pitch invasions and chants from the terraces to 'sack the board', IMUSA and SUAM's campaign targeted the quasi-judicial competition process. Fans found themselves in arenas they never thought they would have experienced. There were none of the public manifestations of protest which the media lap up so readily elsewhere and Alex Ferguson was promised that the team's performance would not be disrupted by the crowd (in Old Trafford's stagnant and hushed atmosphere, this was hardly difficult!). However, such a strategy also meant that expert advice was needed and IMUSA and SUAM were both able to call on the pro bono advice of key City law firms, financiers and political lobbyists, all of whom worked for free in support of the cause. The coalition which IMUSA and SUAM forged meant that invaluable resources and advice were at their disposal, albeit still dwarfed by the millions

United and Sky were spending.

What this new approach also meant was that considerable political support was needed. Two Early Day Motions were tabled and in all 200 MPs signed them, under pressure from football fan constituents. The key role of the DTI (the Secretary of State retained the ultimate say in the case) and in particular Peter Mandelson, opened up divisions and tensions within the Labour establishment. Labour's courtship of the Murdoch press, its promise to serve big business and close personal and professional ties between Labour and the Murdoch empire lent support to those who thought it was a 'done deal'. Mandelson, in particular, was identified as the key player, a friend of Elisabeth Murdoch and, unlike so many in the New Labour cabal, not a football fan.

However, across the new Labour landscape was also the football-mad wing of the cabinet represented by Gordon Brown and Charlie Whelan, the maverick then Sports Minister Tony Banks, and Mandelson's political rivals such as Chris Smith. Even outside government, there was overwhelming opposition from the backbenches, ranging from John Redwood through to Dennis Skinner; this was co-ordinated by the All Party Football Group of MPs. Following Mandelson's referral of the bid (he is thought to have seen nothing wrong with it, and saw the MMC as means of proving his neutrality in approving the takeover) Labour soon felt the wrath of Murdoch. The 'Gay Mafia' scare stories, the hounding of the All Party Group's Chair, Labour MP Joe Ashton, and the *Sun's* willingness to let Mandelson fall on his sword over the Geoffrey Robinson loan, all indicated that Murdoch was firing shots across the Government's bows.

With new Trade Secretary Stephen Byers now in control of the bid's ultimate destiny, and with a feeling that the MMC sessions had gone very well, things looked considerably brighter for campaigners as the March 12 deadline for the report to be handed to the DTI approached. What the campaign had done was to open up a debate about the future governance of the nation's favourite sport. Ownership questions suddenly topped agendas of fans who had bought shares in United out of a loyalty to the club. If BSkyB were to be allowed to proceed, and if they achieved over 90 per cent of the shares, they would force the sizeable number of small shareholders to sell up. This was SUAM's territory. They complained to the takeover panel about the conduct of the bid - no option for rejecting the bid was given to shareholders in bid documents - and they organised lobbying of the plc's annual meeting in November 1998. Speaker after speaker lambasted the board for agreeing to sell to Sky, with not one shareholder supporting the takeover. As one commented: 'I've got my Manchester United shares certificate on my wall at home. It will not be replaced by a BSkyB one!'

SUAM members started looking into alternative models of share ownership, and of organising football clubs, and began working toward uniting the individual shareholding in

'the campaign opened a debate about the future governance of the nation's favourite sport'

Manchester United into a supporters' trust. SU's chair, Professor Jonathan Michie, arranged two conferences on the governance of football at Birkbeck College at which ideas about mutualisation and fan-owned club structures were discussed. The Barcelona fans' organisation, L'Elephant Blau, told people not only about the good things in that club's democratic structure, but also the dangers of letting one man become too powerful in such a structure. Even Irish dairy farmers were brought into the equation as an example of co-operative publicly quoted companies!

As all this was going on, and as the MMC were writing their report, the need for a re-examination of the running of football became ever-more urgent. The FA lost both its Chief Executive and Chair in a £3 million 'cash-for-votes' scandal at the beginning of 1999. Not to be outdone, the Premier League then lost its equivalents over similar shady dealings. A chasm opened up at the top of football's administration, arguably at a time - with the RPC and MMC cases in full swing - when it most needed clear leadership.

Of course, concerns such as the involvement of fans in running clubs, the cost of tickets and the role of plcs in football are core areas of remit for the Football Task Force, the Government's own body set up to find consensus solutions to conflicts in the game. As a member of this body, chaired by David Mellor, I have been involved in its debates which have seen the growth of calls for the independent regulation of football. The outcome of the Task Force's Final Report will be known at the end of September 1999, but, increasingly, the divisions between fans and authorities, small clubs and large, indicate that division is more likely than consensus; and that the Government will have to choose football's future.

The eclipse of Sky

The conclusions of the MMC's inquiry should inform the future direction of both the Task Force and the Government. On 9 April 1999, seven months after the announcement of the takeover, BSkyB's bid was laid to rest by the publication of the MMC's report and its acceptance in full by Stephen Byers. The MMC's conclusions were that combining the most powerful sports broadcaster with the most powerful and richest football club would be detrimental to competition in the pay TV sports market. In this, Murdoch had proved to be his own worst enemy. His oft-quoted philosophy that he used sports as 'a battering ram' to open up satellite subscription sales and new markets highlighted the strategic value of the merger to his global ambitions. He needed Premier League football; the RPC case threatened Sky's monopoly; and so he decided to buy the most-watched team, particularly strong in the make-or-break Far Eastern market. This would guarantee that he had the jewel in the crown of sports broadcasting forever. As such it set the alarm bells ringing within the MMC for the future of competition within pay TV.

Ironically for many of those involved - and particularly those who watch our football in the flesh, not on TV - the future of the television market was perhaps the least of their concerns. It was enormously encouraging, therefore, that the MMC not only ruled on strict competition law grounds, but also declared that the merger would be against the interest of football in Britain, because it would further widen the wealth gap in the game. This brought on board a whole range of issues. It has an implicit recognition that consumption in football is different to other industries in that you buy a product (the football played by a team) whether it is any good or not, and you do not suddenly switch to another producer, effectively making every team a local monopoly supplier. The report also suggested, amazingly, that the 'natural' concentration of wealth within a market, in this case football, was wrong, and that maintaining as broad a base of competition as possible - a competitive balance - was in the public interest. It also hinted that the future structure of football in Britain was of some concern as was the development of the relationship between club and supporter, but that that was more an issue for the Football Task Force. Whether the Government can now follow this report with action to protect the game from the forward march of corporate commercialism is the question which will determine the future of the game in this country.

As broadcasters line up to take chunks out of football clubs, putting their markers down for a time (probably in 2001 when the current Premier League TV deal runs out) when pay per view and individual club contracts are again a possibility, the BSkyB/Manchester United case identified how important football was to pay TV. However, it also highlighted the dangers of a vertical integration of broadcasters and clubs, a control over TV 'content' as well as supply, and in doing so, should have set alarm bells ringing here and abroad. In an increasingly international market, this debate - over how football and television organise their relationship - is likely to move to the European arena sooner rather than later. The lead which the British government take on this may be vital and the battle in that sense is far from over.

For Manchester United fans, as well, the defeat of BSkyB was a beginning as much as an end. Once the delirium of such an improbable victory had subsided, Shareholders United set about co-ordinating small shareholders with the ultimate aims of fan representation at board level and an increasing percentage of the club owned by fans. IMUSA have taken up where they left off in dealing with some more day-to-day issues such as ticket prices and the treatment of United fans in Europe, attempting to get the re-instatement of the club in the FA Cup, as well as joining the efforts of other supporters' groups to form the Coalition of Football Supporters. What was made clear by the process, however, was that without ownership, support representation would always be lip service and piecemeal.

A season to remember

Looking back, the victory over Sky still seems improbable. But it was an improbable season all round. Five days after Stephen Byers's announcement, Ryan Giggs, with his team down to ten men in the FA Cup semi-final replay, and staring defeat square in the face, picked the ball up and single-handedly trounced the toughest defence in Europe in a dazzling fifty yard run on goal, which saw United through to victory over Arsenal in one of the most memorable matches ever. Seven days later, the club flew to Turin to complete the second leg of their Champions' League semi-final against Juventus, overturning a 2-0 deficit to reach the final. Another week later, and United clinched the title at home to Spurs. With the FA Cup also under the belt by mid-May, the European Cup Final awaited in Barcelona. With a Nou Camp stadium two-thirds full of

Reds, and with Bayern seeing their luck run dry, the super-subs, Sheringham and Solskjaer, pinched victory in spectacular fashion from a Bayern team becoming complacent in their superiority. In a mirror of the improbable victories of the fans' campaign, Manchester United lost for the final time in the same week of December 1998 that IMUSA presented their case to the MMC. Neither was to lose again all season.

However, as in football when a new season brings new challenges, the future of the game and its relationship with television remains uncertain. The MMC's decision may have been ground breaking, but the new competition authority may not be able to intervene if another club - with a turnover below the competition law's £70 million threshold - is targeted by another broadcaster. Furthermore, guidelines are urgently needed from the DTI and/or the DCMS about the partial ownership of clubs by TV companies, such as Granada's ten per cent stake in Liverpool. In many ways the concerns the MMC expressed about the Sky takeover - it represented them as 'buying' a seat at the TV rights negotiation table, for example - remain issues when only a portion of a club is owned. The demands of supporter bodies for independent regulation of football, to oversee and even over-rule the increasingly Premier League-dominated FA, will be a key point of contention. On the European field, Murdoch, Canal +, Berlusconi and others continue their jousting and manoeuvring to dominate the European pay TV market, in which football remains the killer content. How European competition authorities, the Commission's sports directors and football's governing bodies handle this battle will be as vital as anything else in determining the future organisation of football.

Despite these unresolved issues, although the events of that warm May evening in Barcelona will live in the history books and stories for future generations as the first time the treble had been achieved by a British club, another event will also become part of football's history and Manchester United's identity. That was that the club's independent existence was saved, for the time being at least, and that television's dominance of football had its wings clipped for the first time. For those involved in blocking BSkyB's takeover, the treble had become a quadruple.

The legal colonisation of cricket

Steve Greenfield and Guy Osborn

Considering cricket at all levels, Steve Greenfield *and* Guy Osborn *highlight the increasing role of legislation and regulation in defining a future for the game.*

In recent years the law has increasingly become involved within popular culture on a number of different levels: the law has, in effect, begun to colonise leisure. As the leisure industry has developed it has faced increasing legal regulation. For example, within the music industry we see the increased visibility of the law in contractual problems, disputes about intellectual property and control over the dissemination of material. The media too has been increasingly subject to legal regulation of content. The phenomenon is equally marked within sport.

There is a line that the law is now often asked to cross (the touchline, the boundary) that might once have signaled a zone that contained its own laws, and was therefore agreed to be beyond the law in general. Sporting legal disputes take many forms and tend to fall into two categories: *participatory* and *consumptive*. Participatory disputes tend to concern contractual and licensing disputes between players and clubs or governing bodies, contested disciplinary procedures and criminal and civil claims made between sporting participants. Consumptive disputes relate to the regulatory powers that might affect how sports can be consumed - these range from laws dealing with safety and public order when travelling to and attending sporting events, to the increasingly important areas of television rights, ownership and merchandising.

This article concentrates on cricket, and, by looking in more depth at the regulation of both participation and consumption of this most august of games, illustrates some of the tensions and difficulties that legal intervention can have. The article concludes by looking at how the law has shaped the history, and how it may shape the future, of cricket.

Cricket's recent context

The Cricket World Cup, hosted, although not exclusively held, in England in the early summer of 1999, was a qualified success in both sporting and financial terms. The Australian side that ultimately triumphed in a poor final contributed to one of the greatest one day games ever seen (against the Lance Klusener inspired South Africa at Edgbaston in the semi-final) and justifiably warranted the title of the best, most consistent one day team in the tournament. Whilst the English national side failed even to get through to the Super Six stages, in purely economic terms English cricket was a winner, finishing the tournament some £12 million richer. In many ways therefore the World Cup demonstrated some of the inherent contradictions within the game, and in particular those present in English cricket. The event, which was billed in predictable postcolonial terms a 'carnival of cricket', indicated that English cricket is in a somewhat precarious position and unsure of which direction in which to move.

There are a number of conflicting issues and relationships throughout the game, from the lower levels of recreational cricket through the professional game and up to Test cricket, that have to be resolved in order for the game to progress. The game in Britain is in the midst of change that has largely been driven by the failure of the England Test team. The alterations so far have been largely administrative, but have nevertheless been designed to provide foundations to make more fundamental structural changes. English cricket has been searching for a formula to make the national side successful for over twenty years, and numerous reports have been commissioned in search of this Holy Grail. The old Test and County Cricket Board (TCCB), itself a product of political machinations, has been replaced by the England and Wales Cricket Board (ECB) which has taken control over not just Test and County cricket, but also the recreational game and women's cricket. The original setting up of the TCCB had largely neutered the dominating influence of the private Marylebone Cricket

Club (MCC) which had spent some two hundred years overseeing not just the national game but, through the Imperial Cricket Conference, the international arena. Whilst the re-organisation of the administration is now in place, and a new two-tier County Championship is set to start from 2000, a set of challenging legal problems, involving player movement in particular, are yet to be faced.

At the lower level, attempts are being made to adopt a more unified system of league cricket which can feed into the next level, the County game. Whilst this may seem uncontentious, it actually involves a major disruption of existing club affiliations. The perceived need is to create local centres of excellence that attract the best players regardless of existing club loyalties. This has been a disruptive issue in other sports; during the creation of the Super League in rugby league, for example, where it was originally proposed that traditional rivals should merge to create more powerful clubs. It has also been raised periodically in football as a potential solution to financial crises, although it is extremely doubtful that fans would support such manoeuvres. At the same time within international cricket there has been an uneasy relationship between the old (Test cricket) and the new (one day games), with the authorities battling to maintain some balance between these two very different forms of the sport. Within this fluctuating matrix there are numerous economic, political, sociological, geographical and legal influences that simultaneously exert pressures on those seeking to change the game.

Cricket and participation: playing the game

Historically the status of players has been a contentious area, riven by the class stratifications of the industrial economy. Whilst the 'gentlemen' amateurs could freely devote their time to the sport - and were usually given team captaincies - the hired hands, the professional 'players', were paid either by clubs or individuals to carry out the donkey work, the bowling. The whole question of the status of participants was not resolved until 1962 when the pro-am distinction was finally abolished. Prior to abolition, amateurs and professionals would have separate changing rooms, different entrances onto the field and even a distinct method of recording their names on the scorecard. (The problem of player payment has not been confined to cricket. Football confronted the problem in the late nineteenth century, whilst the amateur-professional divide in rugby led to the historic split into Union and League; only in 1995 were open payments permissible in rugby union.)

Meanwhile professional cricketers, whatever their level of attainment, were paid artisans' wages. The relatively low level of contractual payments for the leading County and international players was at the root of the 'Packer Revolution' in the 1970s. In many ways the success of the first World Cup in 1975 sparked the interest in increased television exposure. After failing to obtain the Australian cricket rights, businessman Kerry Packer turned his attention to creating an alternative World Series. Amidst much secrecy he signed up the world's leading players to create three teams. To set up a rival venture to the official international cricket structure without any grounds or players at the outset was a phenomenal achievement; it was also one of the first episodes in which legal intervention began to police the sport. Packer's venture ended up in the High Court in England after the TCCB sought to ban those players, within its jurisdiction, who had signed up with the rival organisation. Following from the case of George Eastham in 1963, which had determined that football's retain and transfer system was an unlawful restraint of trade, the judge ruled that such attempts to restrict cricketers were similarly unlawful. The decision helped the development of Packer's World Series Cricket, which in turn paved the way for enhanced terms and conditions for international players and a vastly increased commercialisation of the game. The Packer affair made it apparent to those within the administration of both the national and international game that cricket would have to respond to political and economic global changes.

Part of the globalisation of the game has been the routine recruitment of overseas cricketers to the English game (though there is, in fact, a long history of overseas cricketers playing County cricket).[1] In 1968 it was agreed that the qualification period previously required to play County cricket would be abolished, and the Counties immediately sought to bring in overseas players to add panache and glamour to an ailing game. Since this influx, the question of the participation of overseas players has been one of the most contentious points in the modern game. Critics argued from the start of this phenomenon that the use of such players has stifled the development of English

1. Carol Smith discusses Ranjitsinhji elsewhere in this issue, pp108-9. Historically, international affiliations were also more fluid with some cricketers playing for both England and Australia.

qualified players (a similar argument is being repeated with increasing frequency in relation to Premiership football). The difference between the two cases is, precisely, one of legal status: with respect to football the majority of players recruited to the Premiership, by virtue of their country's membership of the European Union, have a right to work in England. There are restrictions on players from outside of the EU[2], and this is the position with regard to cricket; the main source of overseas cricketers is from outside the EU because of the history of the development of the game. It will be interesting to see whether the increasing improvement of some European national sides, such as Holland, will lead to the recruitment of more Dutch players (a few such as Roland Le Febvre and Andre Van Troost have already appeared) by county sides, given that they have the right to play here on the same terms as domestic players. Interestingly, in a parallel to the old pro-am division, counties often used to look for fast bowlers to spearhead the attack, but in more recent years some counties have appreciated the advantages of employing a world class spinner. Slow bowlers are able to deliver more overs, a value for money consideration, and are less prone to injury.

While fully professional cricket normally takes centre stage, an interesting development has been the emergence of overseas players within the various layers of the semi-professional and recreational game, especially in league cricket in the north of England. This level of the game has become more competitive, in an attempt to build a more formal pyramid structure. The Lancashire League has required for many years that each side hire a paid professional player (Learie Constantine and C.L.R. James first visited England in such a capacity), but elsewhere overseas players have become a routine phenomenon, even playing for village sides. Such presence, doubtless locally welcome if the professional helps the side to win, has also raised a great deal of disquiet. Previous research that we have carried out, through a survey of amateur leagues, demonstrated a high level of concern about the participation of non-English qualified players.[3] The fear is that the local

---

2. The regulations governing work permits and employment were relaxed after the 1998/9 football season, provoking strong responses from bodies such as the Professional Footballers' Association.
3. See Greenfield, S. and Osborn, G., 'Oh to be in England? Mythology and Identity in English Cricket', *Social Identities*, 1996, 2, 2.

established order is being disrupted by the introduction of 'outsiders'. Some leagues have responded by trying to limit and restrict such participation through a variety of exclusionary means, some of dubious legality, while some clubs have argued that the introduction of such players leads to an improvement of standards and assists, not hinders, the development of younger players. What is apparent is that the game, even at a fairly low level, is becoming subject to greater regulation and control and this trend seems likely to continue. This extends to issues such as player discipline; once players are paid this becomes an area of potential legal intervention. There have been some high profile examples of professional players being disciplined for a variety of activities both on and off the field and, as with football, it is vital that disciplinary sanctions are delivered with the right degree of both procedural and substantive justice. Similarly, at a county level the administrators have always sought to avoid a football-type transfer market amongst the clubs and players and have maintained a very restrictive approach to player movement. This has caused some disquiet, and in the light of the development of the doctrine of restraint of trade, is highly likely to be unlawful. Any professional player who has barriers put in his way at the end of the contract period would be able to seek a legal remedy using both domestic and European law.

One final aspect of potential legal intervention as regards participation is worthy of mention. Many amateur sports have looked warily at the fate of a colts rugby referee who was successfully sued for negligence by a player who broke his neck during an amateur game of rugby.[4] This decision may have a number of potential ramifications for voluntary participatory sport in this country, including the role of the umpire in cricket, whose decisions may be opened for later legal scrutiny via a claim for negligence. The full effect of this decision has yet to be seen.

Cricket and consumption

The consumption of cricket takes a number of forms. Primarily this section looks at the regulation of spectators at professional cricket matches, but also considers the increasingly complicated area of TV and radio rights in relation to cricket,

---

4. *Smoldon v Nolan 1997, PIQR*, p133.

and particularly Test matches. In terms of the law's position in this relationship, the point can be made at the outset that the law, and in particular the judiciary in their interpretation of the law, have taken a benevolent and supportive view in respect of cricket at an amateur level. In a trilogy of legal cases, the tension between tradition (in the form of village life and the village green, embodied by the village cricket team) and progress (in the form of the developer who seeks to change or erode, or 'outsider' who seeks to invade) has been played out, with tradition winning.[5] On all three occasions the judges refused to order that cricket should be stopped because of a complaint from a 'newcomer' who did not share in the village's 'delight' in this rural pastime.

We have already considered the legal position in terms of the contractual conditions of the players, but what of that of the counterpoint to the players, the public who pay to see them ply their trade? The cricketing public consists of a number of disparate groups. First are the County Club members who have paid for what is essentially a season ticket allowing them access to all of their county's home games throughout the season.[6] Secondly, there is the group of people with less attachment that might turn up to the odd one day game, a day of a County Championship match or more likely a day at a Test Match at one of the six Test playing grounds. All these groups are bound by certain contractual conditions when attending a game of cricket, the member by the County Club's own rules and the conditions of entry when they enter the ground, the 'ordinary' fan by the conditions of entry alone. These rules cover a number of situations, but effectively only become pertinent for games with a large attendance - few County matches will have attendances of over a thousand a day, whilst Test Matches may have close to 30,000 people for each day of the game. For Test Matches and major tournaments and finals, many particular conditions are utilised and enforced - and some of these became particularly marked during the World Cup.

The World Cup was promoted as a 'carnival of cricket', but the spirit of the carnival that the ECB spin-doctors had done so much to sell to would-

---

5. See Greenfield, S. and Osborn, G., 'The sanctity of the village green. Preserving Lord Denning's pastoral vision', *Denning Law Journal*, 1994.
6. MCC members are in a slightly different position as they are able to attend all matches held at Lords Cricket ground which includes Test Matches, Middlesex matches (who rent the ground from the MCC), Schools matches, cup finals, etc.

be sponsors was threatened on a number of fronts. In particular the need to make cricket more accessible, lively and colourful in order to attract more spectators, participants (and advertisers and sponsors) to the game was clear to the organisers, but they found themselves in a difficult position when faced with 'tradition' at the County grounds the matches were played upon. For example, during the India/New Zealand game at Trent Bridge, the public address system carried first a complaint that the enjoyment of certain spectators (almost surely members at the ground) was being spoiled by 'excessive amounts of noise on the lower tier of the Radcliffe Road stand' and later a warning that spectators standing up would be ejected from the ground. This was at a time when the New Zealand attack was being assaulted by some wonderful strokeplay from Ajay Jadeja and hundreds of spectators, supporting both India and New Zealand, were revelling boisterously. As David Hopps noted:

> Trent Bridge on Saturday was the day that the World Cup organisers dreaded, the day when cricket's past came clean with cricket's future and admitted it didn't much like what it saw. Like an uptight and overbearing parent, disturbed by the clamour and unpredictability of a changing world, it could maintain the sham no longer. 'I don't like you', said cricket's past to cricket's future. 'In fact, I've never liked you. As soon as this world cup is over, I think it would be better if you leave.'[7]

This attempted regulation of 'colourful consumption' via contractual means signals that the enjoyment of attendance at cricket is increasingly being fettered. The consumption of alcohol at cricket has traditionally been part and parcel of its heritage; John Major once spoke wistfully of warm beer and shadows over the cricket field. Indeed, before the deregulation of the licensing laws in the early 1990s, a British Rail train or a cricket ground were two of the few places where you could actually have a drink between the hours of 3.00 pm and 5.30 pm. However, in recent seasons there have been more and more restrictions placed upon alcohol consumption at cricket.

---

7. David Hopps, 'What's all Tannoys? Just Indian fans at a slumber party', *Guardian*, 14 June 1999.

For Test matches we have even seen outright bans and the closing of bars in the ground, in an echo of football's approach to alcohol in the 1980s. The *Sporting Events (Control of Alcohol etc) Act 1985*, which was mirrored in Scottish legislation, originally set up an extremely penal regime with respect to football and alcohol consumption. This has now been relaxed somewhat, though it is still an offence to drink alcohol within sight of the pitch. Drinkers are corralled into areas designated by lines over which the drinker cannot step without fear of prosecution.

Another common feature of cricket, throughout its history, has been the crowd congregating on the outfield at the end of the match to hear the presentations and congratulate the players; in most county games, the (small) crowds can walk on the outfield during intervals of play, and young people often play impromptu games on the hallowed turf on such occasions. This is in stark contrast to the position within football where encroaching onto the pitch, never welcome, has become a criminal offence by virtue of the *Football Offences Act 1991*; since the *Criminal Justice Act 1994* there is an additional potential offence of aggravated trespass. During the World Cup, complaints were made by some of the participating countries about these invasions and the safety of their players, with calls in some quarters for an extension of the football provisions to cover cricket. Since many of the invaders were of Indian, Pakistani or Bangladeshi origin, these interventions seemed to indicate not just the preservation of traditional modes of consumption but a more active, racist hostility. Such concerns were increased when it was revealed that immigration officials had been quizzing visiting Sri Lankan supporters on their knowledge of the game, in an attempt to prevent potential immigration. This parody of Norman Tebbit's infamous 'cricket test' - which asserted that immigrant communities should be loyal to the test team of the host country - may be, and indeed probably was, an example of the way in which institutional racism is alive and well in multi-racist Britain, as well as of the ways in which legal structures can impact on sporting events. However, the wider concerns over crowd behaviour are not reducible to racism: they are equally, in part, a reaction to the 'footballisation of cricket'. Groups like the (mainly white, male, working-class) Barmy Army have helped to alter fan consumption of English cricket, home and abroad, to a more boisterous and vociferous chauvinism - one appreciated by the players, if not by the cricket correspondents of the broadsheet newspapers.

Whilst the consumption at the ground has undoubtedly changed, for a large sector of the public the only way in which cricket is consumed is via the media of television and radio. Historically, cricket was the preserve of the BBC; indeed both quintessentially English institutions seemed inextricably linked, particularly with respect to the radio coverage delivered by Test Match Special, where the cricket often appeared peripheral to the drama created by the inter-relationships of the commentary team. Test Match Special is as much soap opera as sports commentary, and the players are often accorded less public respect than the commentators, for whom the game appears secondary to matters such as the type of cakes being consumed, the number of pigeons on the field of play, or the state of the Gasometer close to the Oval ground. However, this relationship has shifted markedly in recent years with new broadcasters moving in on the traditional preserve; just as the question of rights ownership was at the heart of the Packer Revolution. A similar argument was played out here as within the village game - the debate between tradition and progress - though with a different result. As the new broadcasters, and in particular BSkyB, have sought to buy up TV rights in order to attract subscribers, it has become apparent that the value of such rights is one of the few marketable assets that sports bodies have to sell. The deep political question has been to balance the power of the rights owner to sell such rights to the highest bidder against the conflicting public policy of preserving the broadcasting of sport on terrestrial television. The terrestrial broadcasters have continually been outbid, and many of the leading sports have shifted onto subscriber channels. The challenge for the Government has been to decide what sports rights are part of the national sporting heritage, the so-called crown jewels, and retained for non-pay television. The argument in support of widening the protected events is an attractive one but the cost is that the sports bodies are unable to auction the rights to the highest bidder and their revenue is accordingly reduced. The rights owners clearly want all events 'de-listed' in order to raise their value even if, as in the case of cricket, the rights remain with a mainstream broadcaster. In this case Channel 4 paid the ECB £50 million for the right to cover domestic Test Matches between 1999 and 2002, ending the BBC monopoly of television coverage. Meanwhile, in a move even more threatening to tradition - to the followers of the cosy soap

> 'concerns about crowd behaviour are partly a reaction to the "footballisation of cricket"'

opera of Test Match Special - Talk Radio has bought the rights to cover the 1999-2000 England tour of South Africa.

The future of the game

The current glorification of the highest levels of English professional football obscures its recent history, especially the crises of the late 1970s-1980s that seemed at one stage to threaten the game's long term existence. Hooliganism within the all-seater modern stadia has been largely eradicated and football has a new, glossy image. Those running professional cricket must cast an envious glance at the marketing of football, which seems to have tapped into a rich vein. Law has played a key role in the rehabilitation of football: the post-Taylor environment is a highly regulated one. English cricket clearly needs to adapt to survive and there are signs of change taking place. The crucial question is what role law will play in this change. With respect to spectators, the game needs to attract more to boost not only gate revenue but also the consequent increase in sales of teams' merchandise. Larger gates will need more regulation and there are signs of this emerging with more pronounced controls over alcohol and crowd behaviour. Even encroachment onto the pitch has been questioned, something that, as we noted above, has been part of cricket culture for many years. Interestingly, during the passing of the *Criminal Justice and Public Order Act 1994*, in the debate about the extent of the provisions relating to aggravated trespass, reference was made to Peter Hain and his role in the 'Stop the Seventy Tour', a campaign designed to stop touring sides from racist South Africa from coming to the UK. As part of this campaign, Hain and others regularly encroached onto the outfields (of rugby pitches primarily) in order to make a peaceful political protest. Members of the House of Lords noted that the types of peaceful demonstration adopted by Hain and other activists would theoretically become criminal by adopting certain sections of the then *Criminal Justice Bill* and doubt was cast upon whether this was a desirable outcome.

So cricket has already been legalised to a large degree; the real question is how much further will such legalisation need to go? The most pressing problem that cricket will have to confront is the issue of player movement. The ECB, in its drive to 'improve' English cricket, has created a number of different strategies, one of which is the creation of two divisions within the county championship. This will inevitably mean that the top players at sides in the second division will seek to transfer into the top echelon of domestic cricket. This in turn will necessitate the ECB to look carefully at its transfer procedure as in its current form these are open to legal challenge. In common with other sports, the issue is one of self regulation versus external legal regulation, and the question for cricket is to decide how far it can put its own house in order without having to resort to the law further colonising the game.

Field sports
The pursuit of the right?
Andrew Blake

Andrew Blake *looks at the way field sports define
the different notions of 'countryside'.*

Where is the countryside?

The countryside exists in the mind of both the beholder and the landowner.
Each can start sentences with 'In my view'; which is one reason for the paranoia
of the Country Landowners' Association over the proposed 'right to roam'. But
the complexities of ownership and control are also displayed in the field sports
which country landowners seek to 'preserve' against the wishes of a majority
they represent as ignorant town-dwellers. Through hunting, land becomes both
landscape and virtual space, cutting across as well as confirming the property
barriers of farms and estates. Equally, fishing and shooting syndicates selling
their licensed use of land to third parties; fox, deer or mink hunters engaged in
what they claim to be vermin clearance; and the ground-doping, ecocidal
practices of agribusiness farming; all cut cross each other, and the actual physical
land, in complex relations of use and abuse.

Fishing and shooting, meanwhile, have left the boundaries of post-feudal
'tradition' (still on the whole inhabited by hunters) and become contracted *rights*,
an aspect of the more general regulation, commodification and corporatisation
of contemporary sport through legal realisations of virtual property which are
as ephemeral, but as enforceable, as music-business copyright. The right to roam
would indeed be a denial of this web of contemporary capitalist spatial relations,
and without a profound rethinking of what 'the countryside' is, and how it is
currently operated upon by the forces of capital and class, it would be a fierce,
and arguably unenforceable, anachronism in a world of commodified agriculture,

leisure and tourism services in which the right to access is paid for.

The estate they don't want us in

Those defending country sports see themselves as defenders of country life as a whole: and, utilising the politics of the 1960s and after, they also see themselves - whether lords and ladies or small farmers - as a new, oppressed minority, suborned by tyrannical townies who want a countryside in which nothing and no one gets hurt. And in a way they are; though we are dealing here with something far more complex than a mere town/country split. Political attitudes to the country are conditioned by perceptions of national decline. The left's attitude to the countryside is influenced by the Anderson/ Nairn thesis, which argued that there had never been a bourgeois revolution in Britain, and that instead feudalism and finance capital had produced an unholy alliance which believed in public school education in the humanities or pure sciences rather than engineering or business, valued 'gentlemanly' stock market gambling, and showed contempt for industry and trade. In this culture, apparently, wealth was created so that its owners could retire to the country as soon as possible, and there hunt, shoot and fish. The Thatcherite right, too, believed firmly in this picture of a lazy and wrongly educated ruling class mismanaging consensus when they could and should have been transforming the national economy. Aspects of this ideology were re-inscribed yet again on 6 July 1999 in Tony Blair's condemnation of public-service conservatism. Meanwhile popular valuations of the rural emerged; they include both the creation of Hardy, Herriott and Cookson 'countries' (a landscaped escapism which hides the real ownership of land), and the more politically aware movement for the right to roam whose public expression in the 1930s actually brought about increased legal access. None of these positions has much time for hunting or other field sports.

Thatcherism (re)established bourgeois values partly through modernising the countryside, both through 'heritage' (commodified leisure forms) and through the new enclosure - the selling of land owned by privatised corporations such as British Gas and BT, and the creeping privatisation of the Forestry Commission. In town and country alike notions of public and private space were compromised by these denationalisations. The Thatcherite decade, in other words, established a view of property and right which is closer to the eighteenth century than the semi-nationalised public sphere of the post-war settlement (including the National Parks). The icing on this particular cake was the 1994 Criminal Justice Act, with its draconian new views of criminal trespass, which reinvigorated the sense of genuinely private land-ownership and its legal protection, and which in turn meant yet more bourgeois pursuit of the remnants of feudalism, as a visit to country estate agents such as Knight, Frank and Rutley will confirm. This is one example of something common in contemporary Britain, a 'retrolution', in which the future (of ownership, in this instance) is presented in the past's terms. The photograph below indicates a common way in which the ownership of the countryside is expressed, through marked paths and legal threats.

Country sports: who says?

Again, the right to roam, however welcome in itself, seems ideologically absurd given the intensification of ownership rights during and after the 1980s. The right to roam, on the other hand, is conducive to what most of us would see as participatory country sports - such as orienteering, fell running, hill walking, mountaineering and (a particular landowners' bugbear) mountain biking. These

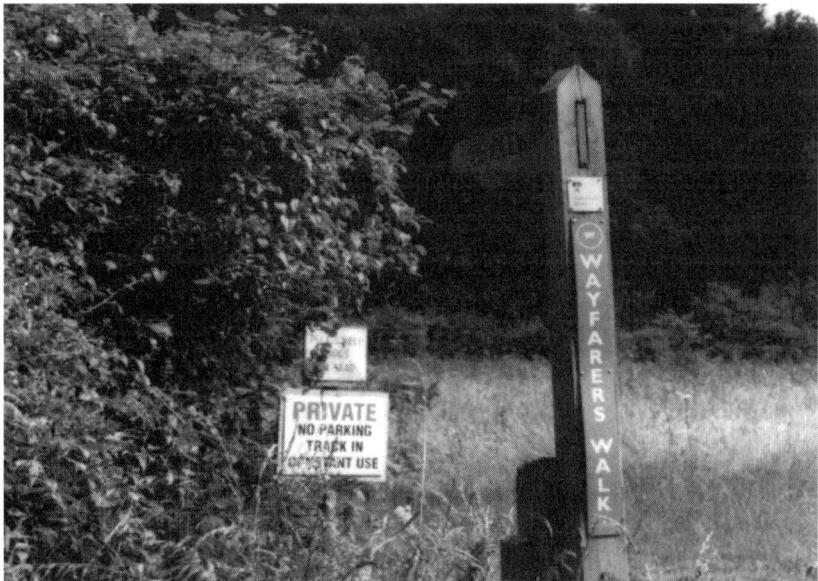

The estate they don't want us in! A typical sight in rural Hampshire, August 1999. Photograph © Andrew Blake.

too both belong in the widest sense to 'heritage' - as inheritors of the practices of nineteenth century aristocratic masculinity - and are commodified activities, served by dedicated clothing firms such as Rohan, and magazines like *The Great Outdoors*, which celebrate the public availability of recreational landscape. Anyone wishing to see a democratic realisation of this notion might visit Sweden, and examine (and use) its cross-country skiing network. But Britain isn't Scandinavia, and activities such as these are not what the Countryside Alliance wishes to preserve. 'Country sports' are presented instead as traditional pursuits of the country-born, an aspect of birthright rather than the legally given (or not) right to roam.

This biologism is only one side of the Alliance's complex position. Field sports' participants and supporters inhabit a world riven by paradox. From Anthony Trollope to Roger Scruton, the more articulate field sports enthusiasts have defended their hobbies by aligning them to the inalienable rights of 'freeborn Englishmen' (though usually refusing the free right of others to oppose them), while professing love or admiration for the beasts and birds they destroy. The Countryside Alliance hides the wolf of retrolutionary modernity in the sheep's clothing of tradition, and you don't have to look hard to see those big teeth. Indeed, the wolf is as likely to eat the feudal grandmother as the Little Red Riding Hood of anti-bloodsports protest.

B
ut the Alliance started by deploying contemporary political techniques against its opponents, to stunning if not quite lethal effect. One of the first actions of the 1997 Parliament was a private member's bill to ban hunting with dogs, passed at first reading by a massive Commons majority, which the Bill's opponents countered not just by lobbying, but by a well calculated use of the politics of mass opposition. The Alliance campaign built on the leftish traditions of CND/ Greenham/ Ecological activism which had become increasingly 'respectable' partly thanks to protests over the export of live animals (in themselves these were a public protest about the unaccountable practices of industrial farming which had produced BSE, currently echoed by concerns over genetically modified crops). The 1998 Countryside March saw over a quarter of a million people in the biggest central London demonstration since the heyday of CND, followed in short order by the abandonment of the fox-hunting Bill through the fiction of lack of parliamentary time. However, this success for the Countryside Alliance was followed by an organisational crisis

comparable to that within the Conservative Party, and driven by similar, interconnected inner tensions; which is probably why Tony Blair considered it safe to re-animate the issue in June 1999, promising that hunting would be banned during the lifetime of the current Parliament.

Those tensions within the Countryside Alliance are profound, and probably irresolveable - industrial farming and game conservation are as unlikely companions as hunting and shooting, which have different conservation needs (e.g. foxes eat pheasants, and if gamekeepers kill all the foxes, you can't hunt them!). But more particularly the class tension within the Alliance produced a number of unresolved issues, involving traditional versus business approaches to field sports, which in turn revolve around differences between the aristocracy and the middle class. Meanwhile farming, by common consent, is in crisis. The millennial situation echoes that of the 1880s: indeed, the very similar crisis (over agriculture and land use in a time of declining prices) which arose at the end of the nineteenth century remained unresolved until the land sales which followed the first world war began to remove the aristocracy from their natural habitat; this created a large number of medium-sized family-owned farms, many of which did well during the subsidy regimes of the 1940s and after, but have recently become unviable in their turn.

There is, in other words, a set of problems in the rural world which should be obvious to all of us who inhabit the hyper-real food-consumerism signalled by the always-available, 'ripe' but tasteless, tomatoes provided by supermarkets which have abolished seasonality by global import strategies. Indeed, these issues are addressed by the Countryside Alliance and its satellite organisations, which, for example, promote farmers' markets as an alternative to the supermarket cartel (for details see the Alliance's website *www.countryside-alliance.org*, and its comprehensive links, which include country-friendly institutions like the RSPB, whose views are in the main hostile to those of the Alliance). The mediated disjuncture between the work and leisure practices of the countryside and the consumption patterns of the rest is reflected in what country dwellers see, rightly, as exclusionary policies. *They are not represented* either by the media or by politicians - who have together handled successive food crises, and more generally, the exceedingly strange relationship between farm prices and supermarket prices, without displaying much sympathy for farming (a tendency reproduced by, among other things, Jack Cunningham's dismissive tone of voice, and the tabloids' enthusiastic demonisation both of GM foods and of those who grow them). It is entirely symptomatic of this genuine problem that in the recent Euro election campaign, none of the Labour Party candidates for my area - which is, geographically at least, both rural and predominantly agricultural - identified themselves as having rural interests.

Nonetheless the Countryside Alliance in its triumphant moment was principally concerned not with the general rural crisis but with the defence of rural sporting practices, and here the representational disjuncture is at its widest. After all, we all eat, and whatever our concerns about quality and safety, most of us recognise that food is produced in the countryside. But we recognise as 'sport' only the games which were codified in or around the 1860s as urban contests with restricted playing times and enclosed areas. In other words, the football codes, representative cricket, lawn tennis and so on were (re)invented *immediately after* the revelation in the 1851 census that for the first time the majority of Britons lived in towns and cities. Even early in the nineteenth century, field sports were an acknowledged aspect of the class war whose countryside manifestations included the Captain Swing riots; only the 1830 revision of the game laws allowed tenant farmers to shoot 'game' animals and birds which were causing damage to their crops. But a generation on, field sports were seen as archaisms. An early attack on fox hunting, by historian E.A. Freeman, published by the liberal *Fortnightly Review* in 1869, simply dismissed it as aristocratic barbarism. This leads us straight to contemporary attitudes - for example the National Portrait Gallery's recent exhibition of Sporting Heroes (discussed elsewhere in this issue by Carol Smith) excluded field sports altogether. There is no place in this pantheon for latter-day Squire Osbaldeston George Digweed's astonishing feats of shooting at live and clay targets, or his equally heroic feats in village cricket (he recently took eight wickets for no runs in five overs, between winning the World clay shooting championship in Atlanta and the European championship in Spain). 'Sport' today, then, in the tabloid press and liberal broadsheets alike, is both urban and professional, just as 'country life' tends to consist of wealthyish townies moving to done-up cottages, issuing forth to complain at genuinely rural noises and smells, to drive to supermarkets for vegetables produced in Africa, or to play that most suburbanised of all sports, golf.

Country sports: who sees?

Television follows the same agenda: there are fishing programmes, but the closest terrestrial television comes to hunting is through coverage of that vestigial relative of fox hunting, National Hunt racing. Even the gentle pursuit of sheepdog trialling has fallen victim to the BBC's increasing post-sportism - in 1998, despite vigorous complaint, BBC2 dropped the popular 'One Man and his Dog'. More recently Sky Sports's voracious, multi-channel appetite for sporting contests has led to coverage of sporting clay shoots, and this year sees the introduction of a clay-target simulacrum of rough shooting which they call 'Man and Dog'. There is no coverage of actual hunting with dogs, or the shooting of birds - no televised 'Glorious Twelfth' of August. This gives a meat-eating nation a strange view of the human-animal relationship in the UK. Some aspects of meat production (i.e. the killing of purpose-bred animals) are occasionally represented on television through the ghetto-slot Country Hour, and tangentially, and implicitly, through the massive number of infotainment cookery programmes; but at prime time animals are seen more sentimentally, through vet programmes such as 'Pet Rescue'. Television casually displays violence against the person, in both fictional and non-fictional forms, but never against animals. This is not to say that television has abandoned hunting altogether. 'Crimewatch UK' and a plethora of 'real-life' police shows featuring car chases, see humans (but, again, never animals) as legitimate targets; it's entirely possible that one presenter of such programmes was then hunted in her turn. This is as close to hunting sports as television gets.

Of course field sports and country living are more generously represented in the conservative broadsheets and in dedicated magazines, upmarket glossies like *Country Living* and *The Field* and downmarket, male-hobbyist weeklies such as *Coarse Fishing* or *Sporting Gun*. Across all these publications the discourse of country sport inhabits and reworks the paradox of all contemporary, commodified sport. Since the object is participation, not spectatorship, the coverage is comparable with that for contemporary 'extreme' adrenaline sports such as snowboarding and hang gliding - which is what they are: adrenaline rushes hit the field-sports participant whether during the careful preparation for the shot in deerstalking, the salmon's tug, or the furious excitement of the run over hedges and fences in fox and deer hunting. But field journalism represents not merely some pseudo-timeless pursuit (most of these activities date from the nineteenth century and were quite as dependent on transport and communications improvements as the Football League) but a set of very contemporary commodities and commodified practices.

In all sports, including field pursuits, capital flows into leisure: through catering for corporate entertainment, and sports clothing and equipment such as saddles and safety hats, rods and flies, guns and cartridges. And through the selling of, precisely, estates: not the superior cottages of the faux-rural *Country Life* but fully-fitted hunting estates with some or all of farms, tied cottages, large houses, grouse moors, salmon or trout streams, and enough woodland and cover crops to hide pheasants, partridges and/or a fox or two. For those who can't quite manage the millions needed for these, the magazines also present what looks at first sight like travel-writing reportage ('A week's fishing in Sardinia'), but turns out to be advertorial for specific field-holiday products, utilising a pragmatic, and inherently corrupt, symbiotic journalism through which the writer's expensive holiday is paid for by the writing fee. Country sports here are a paradigm of sport as corporate exclusivism even more excessive than corporate boxes at Premiership football. Here the ordinary paying punter has no part in the world - though the image of the middle and upper classes at play is confused somewhat by the more plebeian 'hunt followers' (not featured in the sporting magazines, oddly enough), whose enthusiasm for violence is less speciesist than most hunters'. The hunt followers are therefore more likely to be violent against hunt saboteurs. At the lonely end of the political spectrum, extreme nationalist parties, including those in Britain, tend to support hunting on the grounds that it is a 'traditional' aspect of the national culture.

The green death

Alongside the appeal to tradition, the other chief parameter of hunting/shooting/fishing discourse is overwhelmingly, perhaps to the Green-tinged reader alarmingly, the relationship between field sports and conservation. The umbrella over this position is the truism that hunting requires the preservation of game in woodland, scrub, and relatively clean water, and that this prevents the reversion of the countryside to pesticide-poisoned prairies in which, as in East Anglia, streams have turned to nitrogenous drains, with dangerous consequences for the human water supply as well as the fish. The most prominent national game shooting organisation, doubtless with an eye to lobbying tactics, recently renamed itself the British Association for Shooting and Conservation; less hypocritically, it helps to fund the Game Conservancy, which conducts £1.5 million of research annually into topics such as the type of ground cover and crops suitable for the raising of game, which can aid cash-strapped farmers' diversification by encouraging them to farm with a more ecosensitive and biodiverse approach, and then make money from the selling of shooting and fishing rights. Predictably, however, these organisations' views on what could and should be conserved are, er, conservative: their response to continuing public pressure for the preservation of birds of prey is hostile, and the presence of escaped wild boar in Kent is regarded askance, while ecologists' proposals to reintroduce wolves, bears, lynxes and even the humble beaver into the Scottish countryside have been greeted with furious incredulity - but, oddly, with very few suggestions that powerful beasts of prey might provide sport for the hunter in their turn, as they continue to do in East Europe.

While the sale of rights remains a prime motivating factor in this retrolutionary discourse, 'conservation' could, thanks to this timidity, also be read as green-tinged regression - working for the preservation of a tame, post-feudal but pre-agribusiness countryside, coppiced, spinneyed, hedgerowed, iconicised and fetishised despite its historic formation - or more accurately, given the class location of that formation, because of it. 'Sportsmanship' meanwhile is defined through an equally tame notion which involves not the human bravery displayed in the medieval wild boar hunt, the big game hunting which accompanied the imperial project in early twentieth century Africa, or the contemporary Spanish bullfight, but instead a Clintonesque view of the killing of the enemy with no risk to the self: the culling of deer, the control of 'vermin' such as foxes and mink, or the slaughter of purposely-bred game birds. These are the practices of people who identify themselves as (British) gentlemen and ladies, and like all country sports they are suffused with national, gender and class distinctions. Many women hunt on horseback; and many more women shoot game than take part in the more plebeian clay pigeon shooting. Meanwhile the more democratic-masculine French and Italian mass-destruction of migrating songbirds is denigrated as Other, 'unsporting', and destructive rather than conservationist. British commentators earnestly discuss ways of encouraging the performance (i.e. flight in relation to guns) of the redleg partridge, or the declining numbers of grouse in relation to predatory raptors, with a willing acknowledgement of the paradox that they must first conserve that which they wish to kill. But they also defend hill farming, and the hunting and shooting which controls the foxes that are a threat to hill sheep: they defend, in other words, as well as grant-aided animals nobody wants for food or wool, the picturesque but poverty-level human lifestyle of the hill farmer.

Country sports: who does?

A recent magazine front cover featured a profile photograph of Sophie Rhys-Jones, then about to be married to Prince Edward. Mouth half open and gazing intently up and to the right, surrounded by greenery, she cradles in her arms a thing of beauty - an engraved side-by-side shotgun; the magazine in question is the July 1999 issue of the *Shooting Gazette*. For all we know, looking only at the cover, Rhys-Jones is about to end the life of a pheasant; in fact the photo was taken on a charity clay shoot, co-sponsored by Jeep and *Hello!* magazine, in which one hundred young, white, middle and upper-class women, including a fair sprinkling of 'celebrities', raised £80,000 for breast cancer research.

There are some 700,000 shotgun licence holders in the UK, a figure which is in gradual decline thanks in part to the lack of police enthusiasm for private ownership of such weapons. Many licencees shoot clay targets only; most shoot game as well, using clays to keep their eyes in during the close season. Shooting is striated by the class differences signalled by the shotgun itself: new or used, handmade game guns can cost as much as a suburban semi, while equally efficient factory-made guns can be bought new for less than £1000. Similarly, while opportunities for shooting pheasant, partridge or grouse during the season, if available, retail at several hundred pounds per day upwards, pheasants are often bred and shot by syndicates which are cheaper to join, if more exacting in their requirements of members. Common estimates are that over 12 million pheasants per year are bred, released and shot in Britain.

Clay pigeon shooting is more democratic-masculine; indeed its real popularity dates from the Captive Birds Act of 1922, when the semi-rural working-class pursuit of live-trap pigeon shooting was banned (despite a petition in the sport's favour with over a million signatures). Though this was perhaps the last vestige of the anti-popular-sporting legislation which had banned bull running and dog fighting in the 1840s, the new ban on the use of lead shot for wildfowling, from

September 1999, is also apparently against a relatively cheap, 'working man's' rural pastime (substitutes for lead shot are far more expensive). It is hard to argue that shooting live game is only the resort of the privileged, but equally hard to argue that most of it isn't. It is also hard to argue that shooters deprived of live game could not turn to the often exacting disciplines of clay shooting - which, because of the 'kill' when the clay target is hit and breaks, is a more genuine simulation of a field sport than drag hunting is of fox hunting.

After the house: a new country?
The Home Office Select Committee of the House of Commons is scheduled to begin a new enquiry into air rifle, rifle and shotgun ownership. A common lobbying position, most prominent in Scotland, is that no one who is not directly involved in vermin control should be allowed legal possession of a projectile weapon. The assumption among field sports devotees is that the changes, now in process, to the current House of Lords will clear the way for a new hunting bill, though this may be strict control rather than outright ban. It is also assumed that the new Scottish Parliament will outlaw hunting with dogs altogether, and may also try to control private ownership of rifles and shotguns, quite independently of moves at Westminster; and that shooting game will be next on the list when hunting is abolished. Very few people think that fishing - indulged in by some five million Britons - is under immediate threat.

All this leaves some difficult questions. Will the march happen again, and if it is as successful as that held in 1998, will New Labour listen? Are we to have the kind of democracy despised by John Stuart Mill - the tyranny of the majority - or the kind of proportionality implied by proportional representation and the ticket politics of the Third Way? Could the Government try to differentiate positively among feudal owners, entrepreneurial gamelords, and everyday country folk - in which case perhaps it should subsidise non-lead cartridges for wildfowling? Could there ever be People's country sports which involved the torture and killing of animals? In any case, it seems that New Labour is going to ban at least some things very large numbers of people want to do, and then somehow enforce the ban. But whether it does so or not, it's going to have to think much harder about the countryside. And its representation.

p.s. Towards a genetically modified hunt?

As this article was being completed, Greenpeace activists caused what a spokesperson for agrochemical firm Agrebo called 'trespass and criminal damage' to a field of genetically modified (GM) oilseed rape. Jack Cunningham, this time taking the position of the farmer's friend, characterised this intervention both as 'criminal damage to other people's property' and as a 'minority view', complaining that if there are no GM crops in Britain, Britain would have no input into their world development - and implying that this is of itself a bad thing. It immediately occurred to me that a landscape strewn with genetically modified, and therefore *patented* crops, might well contain herbicidally and pesticidally resistant game animals, equally genetically modified and patented. It would be hard to argue that such creatures had natural, or any other rights. Oh yes, we need to think very hard about the countryside, and its futures.

My thanks to George McKay and Alasdair Spark for help in the preparation of this article.

Taking the punches

Gemma Bryden

Gemma Bryden *remembers her first boxing triumph.*

When I first stepped into the ring I was terrified. I had been training as a kickboxer for six months but nothing had prepared me for the moment when my name was called. No backing out now. I clambered up into the blue corner, fighting the panic rising in my stomach. Quite simply, I was putting myself in a situation where I was going to get hurt. The gloves were thrust onto my hands, my glasses were removed and my gumshield rammed into my mouth. My heart was pounding so loud that I could not hear what my trainer was telling me. Three of five senses were AWOL, and the other two in overload - all I could smell was the rancid aroma of stale sweat on the canvas and all I could taste was fear. My trainer landed a few bear cuffs around the side of my head, a reminder to keep my hands up. I glared at him without focusing, not listening to a word this huge man was telling me, instead cursing him under my breath for arranging this fight, sure I was not ready.

The referee called us both to the centre. I tried to walk tall, with shoulders back, meeting my opponent's glance squarely, but all those sleepless nights imagining this moment took their toll. It was hard to lift my hand to touch gloves, so how was I going to smash this person in the face? I walked back to my corner and turned to face my opponent, settling into a loose stance. As the bell rang, the sporting magic worked - in true Pavlovian fashion everything changed and all that training took me over. My muscles tightened, my hands came up, fear giving way to an adrenaline high. I moved forward flashing up a double round kick to the head while rolling under a jab. I came back up too squarely and in a moment of perfect clarity saw a cross snap out. That first punch was sweet. It smashed my bottom lip into my gum shield. The plastic held, my lip did not, but the taste of blood mingled with relief to produce a unique sense of euphoria. I had been hit with a serious punch, and I could take it. She did not land another clear punch in the first round.

During the second round I eased up, fatigue descending upon me like a cartoon weight. I let my guard slip and took a sturdy side kick to the abdomen. I sucked up the pain and nausea and pushed hard, shoving her up against the ropes, jabbing constantly, working the head and face, forcing her to leave her gut open. Once I saw the space I planted a square front kick just under her ribs before escaping without taking any further damage. Tiredness was claiming us both, but knowing there were only seconds to go we tussled clumsily. The last few blows were not pretty and not strictly legal. My opponent's kicks were falling low and fighting close she heel-kicked my knee. Following through on a well timed upper cut I caught her with an elbow to the solar plexus. I just wanted to win.

My opponent was doubled over as the bell rang and the strangest five minutes of my life were over. My opponent and I embraced; she still felt coiled and sharp with a beautiful muscularity to her form, and I hoped I felt the same to her as we shared a moment of genuine affection and admiration. Back in my corner I struggled for breath as gloves and mouthguard were removed. Water was sprayed into my mouth and I spat blood into the bucket. Once I had my hands back I tentatively checked my face. My trainer caught me doing it and laughed at me. Relieved to find everything still where it should be I granted the big man a smile that gave way to a wince as my lip cut opened a little wider.

The referee called us back into the centre to announce the decision. My hand was raised and a trophy thrust into it. I embraced my opponent again before turning to the crowd and relishing my win. No victory since has been so sweet, not even winning a national title. That first fight, learning that I could take a punch, was the most important lesson I ever learned.

Making faces
When socu-soap was young
Steve Hawes

From Billy Wright to Ian Wright, Steve Hawes *charts the birth of the football personality.*

The tenth annual Birmingham Theatre conference recently devoted a morning to a discussion of soap opera on television and radio.[1] More or less playful anecdotes were swapped, as they usually are, about characters in soaps - as if they were real. Janelle Reinelt, former editor of *Theatre Journal,* noting the familiarity with which conferees were able to muse on Shula's rush of blood - not to mention Barbara Windsor's unmentionables - suggested that in knowingly eliding character, actor and person, we were being '...' She paused before pronouncing a word which neither Word's spellcheck nor the *Shorter Oxford* acknowledges, but which must have played frequently on the lips of Jean Baudrillard as surely as it did on those of Marcel Mauss before him. We were being '*ludic*'. Playwright Stephen Jeffreys was moved to admit that he had, until that moment, felt remote from the discussion since he (almost) never watched soaps: but then he realised, as a long-term Highbury season ticket holder, that he had for years been engaged by soap opera of a kind. He had thought - until this moment of illumination - that he had merely been indulging his laddish tribal instincts. But now, as he contended with the giddying thought 'that Ian Wright might be a real person', he realised that he was 'simply being *ludic*'. Like all good jokes this has a ring of truth about it. Indeed, were it delivered straight-

---

1. 'Losing the Plot', a colloquium on narrative, The Manor House, University of Birmingham, 30March - 1 April 1999.

faced, without the inverted commas of irony by which the jester denies his own purpose, we might have nodded sagely: not as post-modernists reflecting on signifiers which *are* and *are not* at one and the same time, but as assembled observers of ritual suddenly aware that our interlocutor is indicating the ley-line of significant pattern. The question: 'When does a person become a personality?'; the answer, 'when s/he has an identity in more than one medium at once: art *and* life'. Or, one might add, two separate art forms, like dance and drama, something which the choreographer Kenneth Macmillan exploited in his work, notably with Lynne Seymour.

O r *sport* and life. Sportspeople became personalities - actors in more than the drama played out on track or field - at about the same time they began to acquire agents. The timing varied from sport to sport and was partly related to the sportpersons' capacity to endorse commercial products. Cycling in Europe, baseball and boxing in America, led the way in the 1930s in establishing athletes as, literally, 'faces'. The rule that interests us here is that the further removed the product was from their sporting activity, the bigger, by definition, the personality rating. Sam Snead's signature on the head of golf clubs might have had the power to persuade specialist purchasers to part with their money: a broader narrative put Denis Compton's face on Brylcreem posters.

Sporting personalities

Soccer stars were relative latecomers into this game. In England it required the players' release from maximum wage contracts in the early 1960s before they emerged as off-the-field personalities. The few exceptions before then each had a ready-made narrative which took its bearer from the back to the front pages of national newspapers. In the 1940s and 1950s Len Shackleton, 'the clown-prince' deemed 'too clever by half', appeared occasionally on the music hall stage; there was Bert Trautmann, the former POW who broke his neck in the FA Cup Final and, displaying Teutonic valour, played on. But their contemporaries, for all their footballing skills, were distinguished off the pitch by self-effacing uniformity. The 1950 England line-up of Williams, Ramsay, Aston, Wright, Hughes, Dickinson, Matthews, Mortenson, Milburn, Bailey, and Finney were ready to bow their heads and hurry down the tunnel at the end of every game, scarcely pausing to acknowledge the applause. No hint of anything ludic there. Even Billy Wright, who became captain, won a hundred caps and married a Beverley Sister, was the model of the modest, unassuming athlete.

But once footballers began to negotiate individual contracts - once they began to acquire agents and, as often as not, a ghost writer for their newspaper column - it started to change. There is a telling comparison between the Manchester United side brutally eliminated from the 1958 European Cup by the Munich air crash and the one which won the competition ten years later. Whereas the former, the Busby Babes, were distinguished off the pitch by nothing so much as their age, the latter contained a few mavericks whose manner on *and* off the pitch demanded acknowledgement of their individual personalities - among them Pat Crerand, Denis Law and especially George Best. For a few years Best lived as if a pop star. He *lived* a 'lifestyle', the popular press avidly detailing the cars, the bars and the 'birds' which defined it; and he *purveyed* one: he not only sported the latest fashions, he opened a boutique and, next door to it, a hairdresser's.

When this change came, television - unlike the press - was strangely slow to react. The football magazine shows of the 1960s and early 1970s were scarcely magazines at all. They didn't carry feature items, and restricted coverage to team news and predictions of the following Saturday's match results, illustrated by clips of the previous season's corresponding fixture, or discussions of in-form teams in more recent action. These amounted to little more than a montage of moves ending in goals, usually picked up at the set piece, free-kick or throw-in, which began them. Producers, directors and editors of sports programmes - and most of their pundits - still belonged to the maximum wage generation and clung to their attitudes.

Football on screen

A turning point was the 1973 FA Cup Final. Not so much for the result - though it was, conveniently, a back-to-front-page story: second division Sunderland beating the mighty and merciless Leeds United - as for the man marketing the underdogs. Paul Doherty was the son of a maximum wage footballer - Northern Ireland international Peter Doherty - who had abandoned his own less than distinguished career as a burly centre-half after brief spells with Bristol City and Doncaster Rovers, and was operating as a journalist-cum-agent in

Manchester.[2] He wrote for the tabloid press, edited the Manchester City matchday programme, and, crucially, was the agent managing the Sunderland players' 'pool' for their cup run.[3] He negotiated the deal with ITV which put cameras on the coach taking the players from their hotel to Wembley, and also guaranteed access to cameras after the game. The insider's glimpse of the hopes and joys of the players and their manager, which Doherty innovatively put on the screen, shaped coverage from then on. The BBC had been made to look stuffy by comparison - a lesson they quickly learned.

By the opening of the 1973-74 season Doherty had become consultant to Granada Television's sports department. Within two years he was the producer both of *The Kick Off Match* - Sunday afternoon highlights of Saturday games - and of *Kick Off*, the Friday night preview show. He moved the latter away from its team news format and demanded at least two feature items a week. What had to be identified (in protagonist/antagonist terms any drama script-editor would applaud) was the 'match-story': inevitably a personal story. Whose career was to be made or marred? Who was the player's principal adversary? What did he have riding on his performance? What did he have to lose? The question 'How do you feel?' became proverbial. Sports coverage was becoming sentimental: it needed perceivable feeling. Just as, Kenneth Macmillan decided at about the same time, did The Royal Ballet. Over six or seven years, Macmillan launched a succession of major tear-jerkers, *Anastasia*, *Manon*, *Romeo and Juliet* and *Isadora*, which deliberately challenged the remote urbanity Frederick Ashton had instilled in the Royal Ballet - and in the process Macmillan turned the dancers into 'personalities'.

In its search for a narrative line which gave meaning to a contest, indeed which transcended the contest itself, *Kick Off* inevitably courted bathos. The subsequent game often failed to live up to the billing, or the personal drama being pinpointed had more to do with sitcom than soap. The Chester City reserve goalkeeper had played one game, his debut, in the 1975-76 season and had let in seven goals against Ipswich. A year later - it was probably also his birthday - he was called up again to play in the cup and Chester had again

---

2. Peter Docherty was transferred from Blackpool to Manchester United for £10,000 in 1936 and reckoned to be the finest inside forward of his generation.
3. Any player involved in pre-match promotion or post-match coverage charged a fee - negotiated by Paul Doherty - and paid it into a pool divided equally between the team once the whole thing was over.

drawn Ipswich.[4] How did he feel? Well, he was glad of another chance to secure a place. Did he suffer nightmares when he recalled his debut? No he didn't. Did he remember each one of the goals? No, but he could remember Tony Henry's back pass which led to the fourth. Was Tony going to be playing tomorrow? No, he'd been transferred to Manchester City.

Just as often the match story laid bare dramatic tensions which would have otherwise gone unremarked, especially when the story was heroic failure. Bolton Wanderers were contenders for promotion to the First Division for the third time running in 1976-77. A camera concentrated on a close-up of their manager, Ian Greaves, as he sat on the bench for the deciding fixture. The subsequent montage, showing wave after wave of Bolton near-misses etching themselves on his face, required no commentary. The same technique, extended over a full hour, was memorably applied in Peter Carr's painfully eloquent record of Malcolm Allison's ill-fated return to Manchester City. Peter Doherty had talked Allison into allowing the programme to be made.

From close-up to close-up

Match coverage changed rapidly over the same period, and along the same lines. New technology allowed the camera a much closer view of the action and one or two younger specialist directors began to exploit this. Len Keynes of Anglia Television, the pioneer of the new school, soon began to acquire imitators, among them Patricia Pearson, the freelance light entertainment director Doherty appointed to cover his big games. These brave ones cut much more quickly, often from close-up to close-up, in defiance of the grammar of the old outside broadcast directors who required everything to be related to a punctuating wide shot showing almost half the pitch. Though the new style could engage the viewer much more directly, the dramatic cutting imposing its own rhythm, it could also be wildly, incoherently against the play: goals which surprised no one at the game often came out of the blue for the television viewer. For several years the BBC's *Match of the Day* and ITV's *Big Match* would run edited highlights from different games, each covered in radically different style. But the trend was unmistakable: action, yes, but above all *faces* caught in the action. Over the same period, and through no coincidence, the rarer art of recording

---

4. A researcher in the office was briefed to track significant player birthdays.

dance for television evolved along the same lines. Derek Bailey's recordings of Kenneth Macmillan's work - mostly live at the Royal Ballet - is the clearest example.[5] Bailey would plot each camera against the score in rehearsal and then leave his production assistant to call the shots in the actual recording, while he directed his best operator on a wild camera which searched the dancers' faces for spontaneous signs of emotion - or, failing that, dripping beads of sweat. It was a matter of getting 'inside' the dance as much as Keynes or Pearson got inside a match.

The difference was that the ballet ended with a final curtain call. 'The swan is dead', Bailey would announce as the house lights came up. But when the final whistle was blown on a football match, it was, of course, a false ending. It is soap opera - and soap opera works because we treat it as never-ending. Apart from post-match analysis, there was always next week, next season and, when a face's career was over, there was the chance of a return game in the same studios as a presenter. Inevitably now, when television producers cast around for presenters or regular pundits, they looked to players at or near the end of their days on the field. It is unimaginable that Billy Wright could have functioned as a studio pundit; equally unimaginable that Ian Wright could not.

Indeed, it was the rule at the time that the non-conformist player - the one with the worst disciplinary record, such as Ian Wright - made the better presenter. There is an obvious connection between non-conformity and 'personality'. Ian St John - whose Merseyside status was celebrated in football's best joke ('What would you do if Christ came to Liverpool?' 'Move St John to inside-right') and who began his television appearances on Doherty's *Kick Off* - was both. Ally McCoist's other life comes, therefore, as no surprise to anyone who was on Doherty's team. But there appears to be a reversal of the principle in the emergence of Hansen and Lineker as the current generation's presenters. Both had impeccable disciplinary records. Indeed, so spotless was Lineker's that the play *An Evening with Gary Lineker* was created to satirise it. But, thankfully, they have both shaken off their earlier prefectorial image. They have emerged as arch practitioners of the ... *ludic*.

---

5.   *Romeo and Juliet* for LWT (1980), *Isadora* (1982), *Gloria* (1983) and *The Seven Deadly Sins* (1984) for Granada.

Staging the spectacle

Reflections on Olympic and World Cup ceremonies

Alan Tomlinson

Alan Tomlinson *argues that since the LA Olympics of 1984, opening ceremonies have come to symbolise much more than sport.*

Olympic and World Cup screenings

The Los Angeles Olympic Games of 1984 was a watershed in the staging of the mega-sports event, providing spectacular opening and closing ceremonies to assert the superiority of the Western, capitalist, free-American way over the oppressive Eastern, communist, totalitarian Soviet way. The Soviet Union and many of its allies boycotted the 1984 Games, in a tit-for-tat response to the USA's boycott of the Moscow Olympics in 1980 (due to the Soviet invasion of Afghanistan). In this context, the Los Angeles Games in 1984 were a statement of the strength of US ideals, ever stronger in the face of Soviet disruption. Allying Hollywood showbiz flair with USA political rhetoric and ideology, the ceremonies set a standard and an expectation for spectacle that succeeding host nations have felt compelled to emulate or to surpass. Events such as the football World Cup also saw the profiling potential of such ceremonies.

In Seoul in 1988, and in Barcelona in 1992, the Summer Games opened to magnificent ceremonies celebratory of the different levels of the regional, the national, and the supra-national - and simultaneously resonant of some of the central tensions within an increasingly globalised world of sports consumption. Aware that Barcelona was a hard act to follow - 'we're not Barcelona', pronounced one awestruck Atlantan after the Barcelona ceremony, 'but we'll give it our best shot' - Atlanta served up its own blend of myth-making and local cultural celebration in 1996.

The made-for-media ritual and the ceremony surrounding the opening of the events attracted the largest share of the global audience, and doubtless many in that audience must look on in puzzlement at some of the most magnificently trite spectacles in history. But everyday spectacle works most effectively to produce ideological effects precisely when it seems to have an other-worldly innocence.

Go south young man - Atlanta's Olympic symbols

Los Angeles had set the pace in 1984, and ten years later had even hosted (well, close enough, it was in the Rose Bowl, Pasadena) the final of soccer's World Cup. Things were beginning to look like a US monopoly. And of course the Olympics' and soccer's longest-running sponsor, Coca-Cola, had its headquarters in downtown Atlanta. Atlanta didn't want to be subsumed under a homogenising US identity, but how could it be both American and global, *and* follow on at all credibly from Barcelona's historical and mythical spectacular?

At the 'Olympic Experience' exhibition in the city, a build-up to the Games, a letter from the boss of the local organisers, Billy Payne, articulated the pitch to the few browsers (a crowd hugely outnumbered by the queues for entry into Coca-Cola's own theme museum a little down the road) curious to see what lay behind the images of the mascot Izzy and the torch/flame logo. We were rewarded with a call to dream with Izzy, 'our fun-filled Olympic character', of what might be in 1996, 'when the Olympic Games come to the American South for the first time ever'. Sure enough the opening of the Atlanta games had something of the dream about it, in its mixture of fantasy and light entertainment, absurd story-telling and clichéd myth-making. The letter from Billy, and associated literature, were at pains to mark out something - *anything* - special about Atlanta's success and forthcoming challenge. Home-town boy Billy Payne had never travelled beyond the shores of the Americas. Personalising an era of globalisation, he could show Atlanta to the world by bringing to Atlanta one of the world's biggest cultural events. Billy the Dreamer drew upon the platitudes of official Olympic history:

> Our mission is to conduct the Centennial Olympic Games with sensitivity, integrity, fiscal responsibility and commitment to the needs of athletes ... to share with the world the spirit of America, the experience of the American South and the vision of Atlanta ... and to leave a positive physical and spiritual legacy and an indelible mark upon Olympic history by staging the most memorable Games ever ... I hope you will sense the anticipation we feel and return in 1996 for the 'Celebration of the Century' - the 100th anniversary of the modern Olympic Games.

'For the first time in Olympic history', visitors were told, 'the Games are awarded to a US city east of the Mississippi River and the Olympic Movement will touch the American South for the first time ever'. Clutching at historical and geographical straws such as this, how could the Games portray a distinctive and attractive image of Atlanta?

The most representative images of the city of Atlanta must be the Coca-Cola bottle, the archetypally ugly urban landscape and skylines, and the inspiring image of the civil rights martyr Martin Luther King, whose dream was more sincere, more necessary and more noble than anything that went on in Billy Payne's head or bed on a Saturday night. At least the organisers showed some good taste in leaving Coca-Cola out of the ceremonial reckoning - the International Olympic Committee (IOC) still prides itself on keeping advertising boards out of the Olympic arena, seeking to purvey a pure, pristine message of untainted, uncommercialised sporting contest.

The ceremony

The proceedings began with five Olympic spirits - each one a colour of the five Olympic rings, red, black, green, yellow, blue - bursting out of the perimeter walls of the Olympic stadium. The colours represented the five continents, and the stadium surface was draped in these colours as singer-dancers looking like robotic sun-flowers writhed their way through their programme. The amorphous blob of colourful and chaotic dancers, drummers and gymnasts gradually assumed a recognisable shape as fliers descended from the stadium rim, in respective

Olympic colours, and five ragged rings and a wobbly '100' made up of children in white garb materialised uncertainly in the heart of the stadium.

At this point John Williams - long-time score-scribe for Steven Spielberg and George Lucas - brought some cadence if not credence to the proceedings, and conducted his centennial Olympic theme, 'Some of the Heroes', whilst the figure 100 re-shaped into a dove of peace. The participants left the stadium for all the world like a drug-crazed exodus of refugees, and the stage was now set for Billy's biggest buzz. Bill Clinton walked into the arena, and up to IOC President Samaranch and Billy himself. Twilight was falling as Clinton was trumpeted in to the US national anthem, and six fighter pilots executed a spot-on fly past. An Atlanta Welcome Wave gave all present a slice of the action. Atlantan culture was now centre stage. Mixed race gospel singing, frenetic aerobic dance (Jane Fonda is a local celebrity, remember), and cheerleaders were illuminated by the headlights of pick-up trucks which had rumbled into the stadium.

The pace slowed as locally-born Gladys Knight sang the anthem of the state, 'Georgia on My Mind', and a sequence revolving around Gershwin's 'Summertime' was offered as a 'tribute to the beauty of the South, its volatility of climate, its history, spirit and culture'. An elaborate dance drama set to a haunting aria then symbolised the birth of the South, issuing from the new day generated by the meeting of the moon and the sun. The set changed dramatically, with the arrival of a representation of a giant catfish pulling Old Man River and one of his riverboats (no slaveships here). Stilted southern gents patrolled the river banks as 'When the Saints' played, to be interrupted by a violent storm of thunder and lightning. To the recitation of the words of William Faulkner on the American South's qualities as 'something that did not exist before', the Southern Spirit appeared to reclaim the landscape from the storm. 'The landscape bursts with new life' spluttered the television commentator, and a hallelujah refrain celebrated the restoration.

The performance moved back towards the broad Olympic theme, as the building of a Greek temple was re-enacted, the Greek poet Pindar was quoted on the greatness of the Olympic Games, and the set was transformed into a cast of silhouettes of archers, discus throwers, jumpers, wrestlers, and dancers, equally resonant of the Greek statues of the athlete, and of Leni Riefenstahl's cinematic representation of those representations. This truly striking set heralded tributes to de Coubertin the founder, who rekindled the flame of the Olympic idea, we were reminded. The fabric flames came to life at this point, as the first and succeeding Games were represented by runners with flags of the host cities. As the Atlanta runner sprinted to the front of the procession and approached the representation of the stadium at Olympus, the pillars collapsed backwards, a triumphalist anthem blared out, young black women carried the Atlanta flag up the steps, and the interminable march of the nations began. After that fashion parade of participants, Muhammad Ali emerged to light the flame, in a moving moment which yet diminished his world-historical significance and recast him as a bit actor in an all-American showbiz spectacle.

France '98: football comes home

In 1998 the World Cup finals returned to the original home of FIFA, football's world ruling body; but reflecting a Gallic-cool take on the event which only lost its shrug as France approached the final, Michel Platini, co-organiser of the finals, was truly laid back:

> Don't count on me to go into your neighbourhood to organise dancing in the streets. Not everybody feels involved. The Ministry of Culture, for example, couldn't give a damn. We've got no relations with them. So it's true, in many places nothing is planned. In others, a lot of money has been invested.
>
> (*International Herald Tribune*, Paris, 10 June 1998)

Platini could hardly complain about lack of state support, with the new 80,000 capacity, $500 million Stade de France about to stage the opening Brazil-Scotland game. The festival spirit was also bolstered by the celebration of the 32 competing countries at Metro-based exhibitions, on boulevards, and at converted phone booths. The Louvre held an exhibition of sporting art in ancient Greece, the Assemblée Nationale one on Sport et Démocratie, the Three Tenors sang under the Eiffel Tower early on in the event, and robots were developed to play football at the science museum. The official sponsor Adidas made its presence felt at its football park under the Trocadero, across from the Eiffel Tower, where the Jules celebrated in neon was not Jules Rimet, French founder of the World Cup, but Jules Verne, fiction and travel writer of an older vintage. However much went on in the stadia and the cities across the country, it was Paris that dominated the public spectacles, on three days in particular: the eve of the opening match, the ceremony at the opening match, and the ceremony after the final game.

On the eve of the opening match, Paris staged a spectacle that, two years in the planning, dominated the centre of the city as four 60 foot-high robots converged on the Place de la Concorde. The obelisk at the centre of the Place had been transformed into a replica of the World Cup, with a performance stage surrounding it. Seating for VIPs and select guests was constructed on the east side of the square, and 20,000 barriers were placed along the parade routes as more than a million people lined the streets. Bus-shelters were removed, and trees cut back so that they would not be knocked aside by the broad shoulders of the giants, each weighing in at 38 metric tonnes. Following on behind the four figures were 3500 costumed children, athletes, roller bladers, dancers and actors. The mechanical structures of the differently coloured robots were camouflaged by inflatable exteriors, androgynous in impact. In the words of their creator, Jean-Pascal Levy-Trumet, they represented 'the anthropological and cultural origins of man ... The giants are symbols of opening ambassadors of the world population, reminders of fairy tales'. Modest stuff indeed, as the giants trundled towards the obelisk/trophy, illuminating the darkening Paris skyline, impressive at first sight, but losing impact once sighted - and taking so long to complete their inelegant journey. 'Togetherness and universality' was claimed by the organisers as the motif for the parade, echoing the tired, traditional rhetoric of world sports organisations. It was a messy start, for the human participants - including hundreds of gyrating children - showed enthusiasm rather than elegance in their cavortings around the obelisk, and on the elite seating VIPs lacked patience as twilight was joined by light rain. Stuck up in those seats, questioning whether this was really the best show in town, I could only wonder what Juliette Binoche was finding to say on the live television transmission.

In the Stade de France itself, prior to the opening match, spectators were treated to a fifteen minute opening spectacle with 17 evolving scenes. The creator Yves Pépin explained: 'The stadium is a garden, an extraordinary garden [an

'the idealistic universalism of the Parade of the Giants towards the Place de la Concorde on the eve of the event was buried in the sexist show before the final game'

allusion to the famous Charles Trenet song], and when an inspired gardener comes to fertilise it, brings alive a patch of grass, these are the multicoloured dreams in which can be hatched, football's dreams.' A large remote-controlled football was guided to the centre-circle by two referees, and began to advance of its own accord, to the rhythm of the music. A rainbow of eccentric, animated people, atop stilts, their hair bouffed up and tumbling down from the sky, entered the arena. Enormous balloons sprang forth from the heart of gigantic flowers, floating weightlessly across the stadium. 'Magic, childhood, and wonderment lead you by the hand into the dream of football, a wholly public spectacle, simultaneously gaudy and poetic.'

Five small figures attempted in vain to control the elusive ball. More arrived, including 380 cartoon characters (les Rase-Mottes, the hedge-hoppers) unravelling an immense moving lawn. Leaping pixies were propelled into unlikely footballing postures by trampolines, while five vast football balloons emerged from five flowers, more than sixteen metres in diameter. Noisy supporters fell suddenly from the sky, leaping from the rim of the stadium roof. As the atmosphere peaked, there was an explosion: the five giant balloons released three thousand more balloons which floated up, twisting and turning. Everybody - almost six hundred in all - came together for the finale. The supporters from the stadium roof rolled out 32 giant sheets, one for each competing nation, while the little magic ball reappeared all alone at the centre of the grass. 'Now that it is there, the competition can begin'.

Pépin was not fool enough to think that the closing ceremony could compete with the after-final atmosphere, and planned a ten minute ceremony. His 'grand finale' was, in his own words, 'comet-like, a flickering whirlwind of light ... on the pitch ... spread to the entire stadium. For the past month, spirits have been lifted by the footballers. For these final minutes of the World Cup, we aim to lift the whole stadium into the night-time Paris sky.' The ceremony was in four parts: the noise-makers' parade; the race of the joyful ones; the salute to the year 2002; and the lift-off and flight. In the first part, 50 bird-like noise makers whipped up atmosphere among the crowd with oil drums, bells and whistles. In the second part, beetle-like figures spurted onto the pitch as if propelled by a spray of flames, half dressed in blue, half in red. Others joined them, dressed in white, also bursting into flames. The national colours of France blended into this fiery scene, as these technicians of the spectacle operated their individual electronic switches to ignite the self-propelled titanium fountains. For the third scene, French carnivalesque gave way to Oriental elegance as groups of Korean and Japanese musicians accompanied the fire-birds on stilts. Let the organisers themselves make the link, lest the absurdity of the spectacle be attributed to my own authorial tone: 'A stiltwalker in the form of a superb blazing sun now appears in reference to Japan. These stiltwalkers are all professionals, and are able to dance on their stilts while handling fireworks at the same time. It is a flamboyant tribute to the year 2002, from France, organiser of the 1998 World Cup, to Japan and Korea, organisers in four years' time.' The final part kicked off with a single 12-armed stilted figure coming alight in a multitude of sun-like shapes, forming 'a sphere of whirling sparks, which resembles one large sun, a football … or even a planet on fire?' More stiltwalkers with flaming torches on their backs surrounded this figure, and the Joyful Ones (from part two) created more circles, 'a galaxy of stars turning around a central planet; a moving sea of fire begins to turn around the stadium'. Following this, fireworks exploded around the stadium's oval roof, one after the other, faster and higher (this could have been the Olympics!), 3900 fireworks in ninety seconds. The final burst saw 228 sprays of stars and comets light up the sky above the stadium, while a million silver petals fell down into the stadium. The ceremony designers certainly cashed in on the late night schedule of the final, with the accumulating impact of fire and fireworks. Before the final, the French Organizing Committee presented 'Colours of the World', a fifteen minute show presented and produced by Yves St Laurent, involving 300 models from all over the world, 13 dressers, 70 hairdressers, 70 make-up artists, 100 musicians, choreographers, stage designers, photographers and 200 specialised technicians. The idealistic universalism of the Parade of the Giants towards the Place de la Concorde on the eve of the event was buried in this sexist show before the final game. It was quite some spectacle with muscled and macho percussionists on primitive looking red metal drums pounding out the beat to Ravel's *Bolero*:

> The unexpected meeting between two emotions, two energies, two sexes. Haute Couture coming into the glare of the football floodlights. Yves Saint Laurent is paying homage to women in the most virile setting of all. They make out they are in confrontation, and yet this evening, masculine and feminine have never been so close to one another.
>
> (Yves Saint Laurent press kit)

Pierre Bergé, of the company, hailed this array of models from all of the world's continents arrayed in the colours of Yves St. Laurent 'which are also those of France and those of glory'. Bergé continued:

> A world of women to precede a world of men. Elegance handing over to strength. One winner leaving the field to another winner. The men and women who, on that evening, will succeed one another, will come from all countries, will be of all races. And together, each in their own way, they will celebrate the mysterious wedding of beauty and sport. When, in the night, silence sweeps over the Stade de France, when the winners crowned with honours will be like the ancient Gods, when the echoes of their fame will spread to the four corners of the world, perhaps the dazzled eyes of the spectators will retain the image of these women, clothed in the mystery and dreams that Yves Saint Laurent, the magician with the masterful hands, has released. On that evening, a new chapter will have been written in the great book of Glory.

Follow that, whoever has to for the opening match in Seoul and the closing match in Tokyo in 2002.

Seeing through World Cup and Olympic spectacles

There are obvious differences between the Olympics and the World Cup, which affect the nature of the spectacle. The World Cup Finals in France was dispersed across ten cities, and involved only 32 national teams (though this was the biggest ever tournament stretching across more than four weeks). The Olympics, though obviously more fragmented in its number of sports, can concentrate more easily on one central site - *the* Olympic Stadium - and runs for around half the length of the World Cup. The Olympics can therefore claim more easily to be a globally representative spectacle, with almost every nation of the world present, and there is a kind of cohesive ritual tightness to the whole event, with the opening and closing ceremonies comparatively close together.

The Olympic ceremonies also have their own momentum as rituals of opening and closure. They are events in their own right, not side-shows to something bigger, whilst the World Cup tournament has been running for years, in its continental qualifying rounds. World Cup Final ceremonies are preludes to games, and are attended - though controversially only on a proportionally small scale - by partisan fans of the competing sides. Consequently, the World Cup ceremonies are shorter, and have less symbolic resonance than their Olympic counterparts. Both, though, lay claim to some of the largest worldwide audience figures.

Why do such ceremonies matter? They matter obviously because so many people are said to watch them - 2.5 to 3 billion people were claimed to watch the opening of the World Cup. But such estimates can never really be corroborated, and ways of viewing are many and varied in intensity and concentration. They matter more because of how universalising rhetorics of world sport - usually stressing peace, harmony, past-present continuity, rebirth and hope for youth - are woven into the textures of the ceremonies. And they matter because in some cases these rhetorics are little more than fronts for ruthless and ambitious companies, or operate as apologetic justifications for dubious political regimes, or veil the real motives of corrupt land dealers and asset strippers complicit with or close to those running the events.

At the very least the ceremonies usually confirm stereotypes - the sentimental American, the wacky and eccentric French - rather than create inter-cultural and cross-societal understanding. When we know the vast profits that can be made by local organising committees, and by the world governing bodies themselves counting the profits in their cosy financial havens in Switzerland - FIFA in Zurich, the International Olympic Committee in Lausanne - it would be intellectually irresponsible to accept merely at face value the public rhetorics, symbolism and ritual of such events. Pierre Bourdieu has argued recently that 'the forces of great global ceremonies like the World Cup ... can be combated either by caricature (which can ridicule or discredit) or utopia (which can propose alternatives to what exists)'.[1] This need not be an either/or. A critical cultural analysis can seek to both ridicule and reform. Critical readings of global sports ceremonies can expose by ridicule, and so prompt debate around and

---

1. Pierre Bourdieu, 'The State, Economics and Sport', in Hugh Dauncy and Geoff Hare (eds), *France and the 1998 World Cup - The National Impact of a World Sporting Event*, Frank Cass, London 1999, pp15-21.

potential reform of, the public face of some of the most powerful sports organisations in the modern world.

For this article I have drawn upon observational data and documentation collected in Atlanta itself; documentary sources acquired on the basis of investigative research; and, of course, the television broadcasts on the basis of which most people across the world watch the Olympic Games, in my own case the transmission of the ceremonies on BBC network television in the UK. The topics discussed here are among the topics analised in my forthcoming book, Sport and Leisure Cultures - Local, National and Global dimesions, *University of Minnesota Press 2000.*

TOWARDS SUSTAINABLE EMOTIONAL LABOUR - A POLICY DISCUSSION

at the TAVISTOCK INSTITUTE on Friday, January 14

Mike Rustin, *Soundings*
Pam Smith, *South Bank University*
Stephen Smith, *Brunel University*

In the home and in the hospital ward, among debt collectors and frequent flyers, in police 'custody suites', in call-centres, among tour-guides, politicians and comedians, emotion is at a premium.

This conference considers the enigma of emotional labour, bringing practitioners and researchers together to establish policies for promoting and protecting 'The Managed Heart'.

Registration fee £10 before 31st December (£5.00 unwaged) or for registrations after January 1st £15.

We invite participation. Please contact stephen.smith@brunel.ac.uk, (Stephen Smith, Dept.of Business Management, Brunel University, Uxbridge, UB8 3PH) for details.

Ask him, referee!

Wrestling in Romsey

Alastair Loadman

Alistair Loadman considers the place of participant/ spectator relations at wrestling bouts in a rapidly evolving sporting culture.

Romsey appears to be the kind of quaint English market town which attracts only heritage tourism. In April 1999's edition of the magazine *Hampshire*, Romsey is described as 'a delightful old town ... (which) ... comes to a halt at the banks of the Test, and from there ... the Test Way leads across the water meadows to the leafy glades of Squabb Wood and beyond.' In this description, wistful notions of heritage and tradition merge to form a particular kind of Englishness; a kind exemplified by the careers of two former residents of Broadlands House: the 3rd Viscount Palmerston and Earl Mountbatten, whose connections with the world beyond signal the more aggressive aspects of the national past. Of the townscape's other dominant structures, Romsey Abbey, a mix of Norman and Gothic, symbolises this post-feudal hierarchy, and is the largest parish church in Hampshire since it was dissolved as a monastery in 1544. Meanwhile the 150mm Japanese field gun seized by the 14th Army in Burma four hundred years later, under Mountbatten's command, stands in the War Memorial Park, a frozen metaphor for the imperial past.

Yet the town also exhibits the rhythms, patterns and social tendencies which are the stuff of a differently globalised everyday life. In common with larger touristically-defined places such as Bath or Cheltenham, Romsey possesses a duality of spirit; residents co-exist with the manufactured tea-room hyper-reality of heritage culture. There is concern over traffic congestion; the occasional fight breaks out in an Indian restaurant late on a Friday night; Sainsbury's wants to open a new superstore. This is the inhabitants' world: Sky dishes on redbrick houses, pit bull terriers snarling outside the Romsey Tavern, a broken shopfront on a Saturday morning, the stink of urine in the subway at the railway station where crowded trains carry people to work in Southampton, seven miles away. Local employment has changed: Whitbread ceased brewing in 1980, and architects and design consultants have offices in the former brewery; meanwhile the South African born, former England batsman and current Hampshire captain, Robin Smith, has opened Judge's Wine Bar. Far from being frozen in Heritage Time, then, Romsey has been subject to the disruptions and discontinuities, contradictions and complexities which characterise contemporary Britain.

Rumblemania

Early in 1999 Rumblemania, an American professional wrestling format, came to Romsey. Since the disappearance of wrestling from Saturday afternoon ITV (to re-appear as the fully Americanised WWF extravaganza on satellite channels), wrestling has been neglected in media sports coverage, which focuses disproportionately on football, cricket and rugby union. Yet, when over two hundred people attend a wrestling evening, with the age of the audience ranging from 8 to 80, when skilful performers of mainly middle age are the focus for admiration or derision in a youth-oriented society, this is surely an event worthy of our attention. Interconnected structures at work in wrestling carry significance for wider understandings of sport in a televisualised, commodified world: the pre-match hyping of the events; the role of the warm-up man (and it always does seem to be a man) in creating the necessary 'atmosphere'; the communication between performers and spectators.

And yet it is easy to see why sports writers (and academic researchers) find wrestling problematic. Wrestling does not neatly fall into any one category of human performance - neither is it 'purely' sport nor is it 'simply' dance, carnival or theatre. It contains elements of all the above, including physicality, staging, plot, character, choreography, skill, athleticism and rule structures. Further, there is much to be said about the social and cultural processes through which relationships between spectators and performers are forged, and that is the principal reason why interest in the sport has been shown from cultural studies.

Authors working in cultural studies have attempted to locate the spectacle within broader social and cultural frames. Within this common project, however, each has sought to emphasise different perspectives. Roland Barthes maintains that wrestling is best conceptualised as a spectacle in which ideas about suffering, defeat and justice are fundamentally embedded. Indeed, Barthes asserts that the 'Exhibition of Suffering is the very aim of the fight'.[1] Alternatively, John W. Campbell argues for wrestling as a 'mirror of the free market': in the real world, the spoils often go to those who cut corners, lie, cheat and otherwise bend the rules. According to Campbell, no one should be surprised that the 'bad guy' usually wins, because wealth and status accrue to those who are able to bend the rules most effectively.[2] A complementary set of considerations is addressed by Alasdair Spark, who suggests that wrestling constitutes a 'zone of Americanization in British culture'.[3] For Spark, wrestling presents a spectacle in which paradoxes and contradictions over personal and national identity become acutely apparent through the staged and constructed identities of, for example, 'American', 'English' and 'Scottish' performers.

For me wrestling is an essentially humorous activity, in which the bouts themselves constitute the embodiment of irony. I question Barthes' interpretation of the essential nature of wrestling, arguing that comedy is in fact the underlying rationale. In locating the active role of the audience within this humorous matrix, I also take issue with Campbell's claim that 'wrestling fans need not spend any intellectual energy making sense of wrestling'.[4] This patronising view neglects the negotiated meanings which are wrought from the experiences of watching sport. In this regard, Roger Homan is surely right to emphasise the active engagement of the audience when he refers to spectators who 'rise to their feet to protest at the habits of such as Cyanide Sid Cooper of Soho; their participation and influence affords the sense of empowerment'.[5]

I suggest that the relationships between spectators and performers are not

---

1. R. Barthes, *Mythologies*, Hill and Wang, New York 1993, p19.
2. J.W. Campbell, 'Professional Wrestling : Why the Bad Guy Always Wins', *Journal of American Culture*, 19 (2), 1996, pp127-132.
3. A. Spark, 'Wrestling with America: Media, National Images, and the Global Village', *Journal of Popular Culture*, 29 (4), 1996, p96.
4. Campbell, *op.cit.*, p127.
5. R. Homan, 'Private Parts: Ethical Issues in the observation of wrestlers', *Ethics, Sport and Leisure: Crises and Critiques*, Chelsea School Research Centre, Brighton 1995, pp178.

as straightforward as sometimes presented, and humour resonates in many different ways: from the slapstick, exaggerated 'clumsiness' of movements and the feigning of injury, through the obligatory 'good guy/bad guy routine', to self-parody, irony and humorous interplay with the audience. Meanings in wrestling are conveyed through various modes including the bodies and physical movements of the combatants, the staging of the event (lights, music, the garish clothing of the wrestlers and of the officials), and the outcomes of the contests themselves. According to Laurence de Garis, meanings are communicated between wrestlers through the strength or softness of touch, enabling moves to be choreographed to greatest effect.[6] In enacting these forms of physical theatre, wrestlers also exploit opportunities for humour, often at their own expense.

Admittedly, Barthes does not preclude the possibility of humour within the spectacle, pointing out that the wrestler may seek to personify 'the ever entertaining image of the grumbler, endlessly confabulating about his displeasure'.[7] However, I argue that comedy is the raison d'etre of wrestling. The seeds of humour are initially cultivated during the lead-up time, in which the event's promoters set out their wares. The advance publicity in this instance took the form of a black and white mailshot, posted through front doors in my neighbourhood. This prepared the groundwork for preferred readings of the forthcoming 'Wrestling Spectacular'; the process of naming the participants, particularly through the judicious use of pseudonyms and nicknames, conveyed certain (pretty obvious) messages about 'Tarzan' Johnny Wilson and 'Cyanide' Sid Cooper. Caricatured identities, which are essential to comedy, are established through the naming process. In wrestling, as increasingly in other sports, the pre-match hype exaggerates the anticipated conflict through caricature of the contestants. This is important because irony is one of the sources of humour in the wrestling ring, and irony, as a literary/theatrical mode, assumes a reader/audience 'ahead' of the performers. Like the practitioners themselves, we see the moves coming before they are enacted. The advance publicity, and the nicknames, help us to do so.

The press release ('Is Romsey ready for Rumblemania?') offered prospective punters a glimpse into the world of wrestling through a more detailed and vivid

---

6. L. de Garis, 'Experiments in Pro Wrestling: Toward a Performative and Sensuous Sport Ethnography', *Sociology of Sport Journal*, 16 (1), 1999, pp65-74.
7. Barthes, *op.cit.*, p18.

naming of the contestants. We discovered that 'Tarzan' Johnny Wilson is also known as 'the south coast strongman', and that the line up would 'include the burly 6ft 5ins powerhouse Big John Prayter'. These messages underline the centrality of excess/exaggeration and humour/irony to wrestling; the two key devices serving mutually to accentuate the other. The press release also served to educate and inform those who had not been prepared by WWF shows on satellite television about the rules and structures of all-in American 'Rumbles'. For example, wrestlers can only be eliminated by being thrown over the top rope: a radical departure from the usual scoring system, and a much more dramatic signifier of victory.

Contrasting contests

The Plaza theatre is a magnificent art deco building which faces towards Broadlands House. Outside, posters advertise a forthcoming Gilbert and Sullivan production by the local operatic society. On entering the building, we are greeted by an elegantly-attired usher who, reassuring us that we have come to the right place, directs us to 'find a seat through there, if you can'. As we move towards the auditorium - audience still unseen - the hum of conversations grows loud. There is a very nearly full house, and we have to look carefully to find two vacant seats. We walk up steps taking us away from the front row and past many faces, all of whom are white except for one teenage boy who is in the middle of a line of other youths who appear to be 'with' an older man. There is a wide range of ages amongst those present, from primary school-aged children to the elderly. Nearer the front, I notice a wheelchair placed to one side of the aisle. Whilst the audience is predominantly male, significant numbers of women are present; usually, it appears, accompanied by a man.

Suddenly, the house lights dim and the stage is illuminated. The square ring (the area in which the action takes place) is anchored by large, grey metal posts at each corner. Their colour contrasts with the vivid crimson of the apron - the cloth which covers the sides of the ring - and the juxtaposition is heightened by the 'drenching and vertical quality of the flood of light'.[8] The ring is raised perhaps six feet above floor level, with the result that it looks down on the first few rows of spectators, until the banking of the seating takes effect.

---

8. *Ibid.*, p15.

Juxtaposition and contrast are central to many forms of comedy in various media. Past and present television shows provide numerous examples of humour generated through deliberate contrast of different personalities, ages or bodies. Well known performers such as Laurel and Hardy, 'Little and Large', 'Steptoe and Son', and Morecambe and Wise have fruitfully exploited arrangements of these kinds. Contemporary shows such as *Men Behaving Badly* and *Game On* use gender opposites as the basis and catalyst for similar comic dialogue and movement. In wrestling, however, the bodies of the wrestlers are often of similar size, so the differences lie in the postures, gestures, features and 'characters' of the performers. In this way, the wrestlers' bodies are managed to produce a humorous discourse to which the audience responds and with which they actively engage. The evidence of this engagement is most apparent when the audience responds ironically to the irony that is wrestling, as when a teenage boy shouted 'Ouch!' and 'I bet that hurt!' during the first contest.

The 'MC' (Master of Ceremonies) climbs into the ring. White socks peep out from beneath formal black trousers. Relatively small and slightly built, he appears nervous, pacing forwards and backwards as he welcomes us to the wrestling spectacular. He finds it difficult to engage the audience ('warming them up') for the evening ahead and, despite his exhortations to 'put the music on and steam up the volume a bit', the crowd's response is muted. The Tina Turner hit 'Simply the Best' booms around the theatre, predictably, but to no avail. The next part is critical, however, as he introduces the contestants in the first bout, between 'Danny Vincent, from the Isle of Sheppey, Kent' and 'James Mason, from Bermondsey, London'. These two contenders, apparently, are 'two of the brightest young prospects on the wrestling scene at the moment'. At this point, to generous applause, two white men probably aged between 25 and 30 emerge from behind a curtain and enter the ring.

This bout, to conventional rather than Rumble rules, is characterised by conformity. The wrestlers' bodies reinforce notions of cleanliness, conservatism and rectitude. Vincent and Mason are the muscular embodiment of 'good'; each has the 'right' body shape (mesomorphic and athletic) to enable them to play their roles. They are ambassadors for the antiquated sport ethic of fair play, a parody of an era which, if it ever existed, is long since past and clung to only by successive sports ministers and former prime ministers in nostalgic speeches about England's glorious sporting ancestry rather than its parlous present. At the time of writing England's sportsmen are ranked a generous thirteenth in world football, have been eliminated early from the cricket World Cup, had finished behind Scotland in the Five Nations rugby, and had been knocked out of the Davis Cup by two fading American tennis players (the top American seeds having declined to compete).

The bout

The bearing of both wrestlers is upright, their faces clean shaven, and they show deference towards the referee (whom I recognise as a former star of televised wrestling from the early 1970s) on the rare occasions when he intervenes; throughout the bout his authority is unquestioned. As the contest develops, there is sporadic applause and the occasional vocalised offering from individuals in the audience. But, in the main, there is relative quiet and the potential for humour is limited to the referee as, with an expressionless face and an exaggerated show of officialdom, he leans and stoops to 'check' that the moves and holds executed are 'legal'. An outstretched arm towards the wrestlers signifies the thorough (mock) seriousness of this 'checking'.

The contest is characterised by a series of holds and throws from which both wrestlers successfully 'escape' by using technical forms of bodily knowledge - for example, by applying force at a particular angle to release the hold, or by resolving a throw with an adroit rolling action and lightness of movement. There is a considerable degree of skill demonstrated during these phases. The scoring sequence commences with a fall in the third round to Vincent, followed by an equalising fall to Mason in the fifth (a 'fall' is the word used to describe the sport's scoring move, whereby one wrestler's shoulders are pinioned to the floor for a count of three seconds). The timing of their 'escapes' heightens the dramatic effect. In a closely-fought sixth and final round, there are several 'near misses', when both wrestlers just manage to 'escape' at the last second. Finally, as both men have one fall each, the referee indicates that the contest is a draw and we are invited, by the MC, to show our appreciation for both wrestlers 'in what you will agree, ladies and gentlemen, was a great sporting contest'.

Rumblemania finally arrives in Romsey with the second bout of the evening, a Tag Team contest in which 'Superstar Mal Sanders' and Steve Grey (current PWF champions) are pitted against 'Simply the Best, Adrian Finch' and Cyanide

Sid Cooper. Cooper, aged around fifty, with closely cropped hair, a prominent nose and hooded eyes that have seen it all, enters the ring wearing a bearskin-style dressing gown. As he does this, a boy to my left shouts 'See ya later, Flintstone!' - emphasising the perceived Americanness of this contest. Removing his dressing gown, Cooper reveals a leotard struggling to contain a large beer belly. His taller partner, Adrian Finch, has a slightly hunched back, and is remarkable for lack of muscle tone and lank, ear-lobe length hair. Quite simply, he does not look the best. Their opponents exhibit greater athleticism in movement and seem in better physical condition. They are not, however, the demons of the piece, who identify themselves before the bout, as Cooper snatches the microphone from the MC and remarks: 'I've never seen such ugly children in all my life!' This generates some indeterminate shouting from the audience.

Whereas the Vincent-Mason encounter was notable for rule conformity, respect for authority and the deadpan performance of the referee, this bout is characterised by rule breaking and illegality. As such, it constitutes a deliberate usurping and ironic critique of the fair play ethic. In one phase of the contest, Finch pulls Grey backwards by the hair when the referee's back is turned. Having manoeuvred Grey into this 'blind spot', Finch delivers a series of 'punches' to an unprotected midriff. The drama is heightened when Sanders attempts to 'save' his partner from this onslaught by attempting to tag (make brief, hand-to-hand contact) the unfortunate Grey, take his place in the ring and thus put an end to his 'suffering'. Sadly, his partner remains tantalisingly out of reach.

The idea of suffering is further developed when the hapless Grey becomes the recipient of a series of 'postings' - a posting is a deliberate throwing of a wrestler against one of the ring's corner posts with the intention of weakening the back. In this contest, the posting was made more 'effective' by Cooper's sly removal of the post's protective padded sleeve prior to the move being executed. In the arguments which follow and as a final twist to the plot, the referee 'misses' a legitimate tag by Grey and Sanders. Thus, just when we thought it was safe for Grey to recover in the sanctuary beyond the ring, he is ordered back in by the referee to endure still further 'punishment'.

In this sequence of events, the comedy works through the ironical naming of the wrestlers, their contrasting body shapes, direct verbal communication between wrestlers and audience, and 'incompetent' displays of refereeing. It also works through a dramatic device which I shall call action switching. In this process, the 'bad guy' begins a move - e.g. an intended posting - but his opponent works around the move and switches the action so that it is the 'bad guy' who eventually receives the posting. This device also fulfils the function of signifying 'payment' for wrongs previously committed (another important part of wrestling), and serves to increase the intensity of audience participation - though it is not unidirectional. When Cyanide Sid Cooper received 'his second, and final, public warning', a girl of about eight years stood up in front of me and raised both arms aloft, fists clenched in triumph, while a middle-aged man boasting an Elvis ducktail hairstyle, who had earlier been heard to call 'Come on, Sid!' remained motionless in his seat.

Theatre or sport?

It may be that all sport is tending towards wrestling's hybrid theatricality. The technique of preparing the viewer is widely used across other media-sport constituencies: in the televised lead up to the 1999 international rugby union championship, commentator Bill Maclaren breathlessly announced: 'Five Nations, One Spectacle'. Furthermore, Maclaren made explicit reference to the 'national characteristics' of the teams taking part (the 'durability of the Scots', for instance). Well before the action begins, in other words, viewers are alerted through such patterns of naming to preferred readings of the event. The April 1999 match in this series between Wales and England provided further evidence of the collapsing boundaries between theatre and sport - and of the sense of nostalgia which sometimes tinges these events, as Tom Jones, a pop star whose heyday was the 1960s and 1970s (also the halcyon years of Welsh rugby), and Max Boyce (a comedian/songwriter of the same era) led the crowd in a pre-arranged burst of 'community singing'. Less dramatically, spectators at Dean Court (the home of soccer club AFC Bournemouth) are offered a weekly pre-match diet of 'witticisms' broadcast over the public address system, whilst an employee dressed up as a bear cavorts along the touchlines. Both warm-ups try to create a crowd response of the sort wrestling takes for granted.

The wrestling crowd is fully aware of its role in the evening's entertainment and responds appropriately. Spectators are enmeshed in the comedy that is wrestling, and to preclude ironic participation by the crowd on the grounds that they are 'hardly sophisticated' is both patronising and short-sightedly fails to take account of the importance of the audience's feedback in the construction of the event. As the divisions between sport performers and spectators dissolve, communication between the two parties becomes increasingly noticeable. In this dialogue, performers utilise signifiers of various kinds to encode messages to the crowd, whilst the crowd reciprocates with vocalisation and gesture to produce a collective sports event, a product forged out of the alliances between spectators and performers. Recent televised coverage of World Cup cricket matches and Wimbledon tennis underlines the increasingly active nature of crowd participation in sport; with audience props such as flash cards employed both to interpret and emphasise key points in the contests.

The significance of professional wrestling is that, despite its ambivalent status as competitive sport, it illustrates vividly some of the characteristics and features of modern professional sport. It may become more appropriate to speak in terms of sportstainment - the frank term used by the World Wrestling Foundation (WWF) to indicate that it is a meld of the two. Maybe this is the future of all sport. Maybe, too, watching wrestling at the Plaza is more 'real' than watching yet another football match on television because it is live. It is also both local and 'global' - in its adoption of an American format. Professional wrestling tells us something valuable about the performer/ spectator relationship in a changing form of popular culture, and in a moment when the meanings of sport itself are evolving rapidly.

Thanks to Paul Key, Nigel Tubbs, Alasdair Spark.

Notes on camp
New Labour and the body(building) politic

Adam Locks

Adam Locks considers the parallels between bodybuilders' construction of a 'new' image, and the controlled re-invention of New Labour.

The Conservative Party seems, increasingly, to mirror English cricket. Despite the fact that the petit-bourgeois John Major's obvious passion for the game helped literalise this fusion between sport and party, both continue to signify the upper classes, public school, and a preference for the old and established. Perhaps more damagingly, both also signal a dislocation from Europe, a playing by the rules of white patriarchy, and most importantly the current failure of that mixture.

Despite the freezing over of the Cool Britannic attempt to be young and hip, New Labour might want to be seen, by contrast, as football's party. Indeed, despite the refusal of Rupert Murdoch's bid for Manchester United, the media-led postmodernisation of top-level football in Britain seems homologous with the New Labour 'project'. But this is altogether too obvious and easy a game. A less likely corner of the world of sport provides a more appropriate metaphor: let us compare New Labour to bodybuilding. Each is focused upon ideas of re-invention and change; further, each prioritises *style* over *content*, and *form* over *function*, a claim that has frequently been made against the Government since New Labour's election victory in May 1997. Bodybuilding, I argue, is not only the perfect sportification for New Labour because of the party's preference for style over substance, but also because of its partiality for artifice and hence, I suggest, unintentional 'camp'. As a metaphor for New Labour, bodybuilding is body politics without polity.

Bodybuilding is above all an art of transformation, using the structures of the body to produce a polished surface which apparently signifies an embodied power, but which can only express that power through poses. Bodybuilding would seem, then, to be an aspect of that dislocation between form and function which (without falling into the catch-all of 'postmodernism') we might associate with 'pop art'. Emerging during the 1960s, the pop sensibility rejected depth and focused instead on surface, and as Leon Hunt suggests, 'elicited a new way of looking'. The Labour Party's preference for style, noticeable throughout the first two years of office, seems to offer up a 'pop' sensibility into the realm of British politics, in which New Labour's focus on image has instigated a new way of voting.

As such, the New Labour/Cool Britannia project can be associated with the rejection of high-art modernism which characterised such movements as pop art. In the early twentieth century, Pablo Picasso's experience of seeing examples of African sculpture drastically affected the methods of representation in western art. Influenced by non-Western aesthetics, much modernist art rejected the agreed post-medieval codes of direct representation. Such works renounced not only previous notions of individual identity, but also the aesthetic *ideals* of beauty which were, in the main, inherited from Classical models. Picasso, who directly before *Les Demoiselles* had based his 'pink period' work precisely on vase painting and sculpture from Greek antiquity, now embraced a very different aesthetic, and through his influence, notions of beauty and perfection via direct representation were discarded. Throughout a post-war western Europe dominated by an antirealist aesthetic in the plastic arts, *modernism* has been the primary narrative: abstract images are privileged over mimetic ones and, especially, a mimesis based upon classicism. In these terms, current artists such as (New Labour fan) Damien Hurst and Cornelia Parker continue a tradition of modernism that started with Impressionism and continued through Cubism, Futurism, Dada, Constructivism, Surrealism, Abstract Expressionism and Conceptualism. Much of this art attempts the shock of the avant-garde, an iconoclastic imperative developed early in the twentieth century. The remnants of the Classical tradition of idealised bodily representation have been firmly left to popular culture: comic-books,

Hollywood movies, photographs of supermodels - and the practice of bodybuilding.

However, the continued renunciation of European Classicism as an ideological aesthetic is also due, in part, to its fascist and Stalinist appropriation during the 1930s. The classical tradition stemmed from ancient Greek celebration of a youthful, athletic masculinity which represented perfect self-development and self-discipline through figures of idealised manhood such as Apollo and Hercules. This cult of physical perfection re-emerged in Nazi Germany where youth, vitality, and power were fetishised through ideal representations of the male body. Muscularity became a prime focus for such idealism, its painted and sculptural representations usually in a kind of pseudo-classical kitsch - Rubensian musculatures hysterically celebrating the possibility of a new Nordic race. Meanwhile through the 'socialist realism' of Communist art, the idealised body was also conflated with elements of totalitarianism.

In post-cold war Russia, the New Academy of Fine Arts in St Petersburg has recently exhibited paintings (by such contemporary Russian artists as Ivan Dmitriyev and Georgy Guryanov) of heroic, muscular males. Such paintings as Dmitriyev's *Dream* (1994) evoke the ancient Greek representations of the male body, celebrating nationalism and masculinity, while deliberately echoing the state-sponsored realism advocated during the 1930s and after. Such neo-classical Russian art breaks with the modernist engagement with non-Western aesthetics in favour of an imagined Classical European past which has little to do with Russia's actual past - or present. (It is worth pointing to a parallel with Cool Britannia's location in a Britpop/pop art aesthetic, which as Jeremy Gilbert has pointed out implicitly relocated contemporary multicultural Britain in an imagined white, monocultural 1960s.[1])

But though the classical tradition does not of itself signify totalitarianism, it is never politically neutral. During the Renaissance, the art of classical antiquity was revived, most famously with Donatello's *David*, Monegna's *Sebastian*, and Michelangelo's *David*. As Margaret Walters points out, there was a political motivation for the popular rise

1. J. Gilbert, 'Blurred Vision: Pop, Populism and Politics', in A. Coddington and M. Perryman (eds), *The Moderniser's Dilemma. Radical Politics in the Age of Blair*, Lawrence and Wishart 1998, pp75-90.

in depicting muscular males during this time:

>...[A] city like Florence, with its long-established trading and financial empire, its cycles of boom and bust, its constant struggles to survive against other cities, put a new premium on aggressive individualism, mobility and competitiveness ...The classics are invoked to validate the qualities needed for success in early mercantile capitalism; those qualities are seen as defining a man...[2]

If we accept this insight, then it would seem that the re-emergence of neoclassical muscularity during the Renaissance is less like 1930s totalitarianism than the similar emergence of such figurations during the 1980s where, again, 'aggressive individualism' was the celebrated mode of being within the market economy. The idealisation of muscular masculinity was revived principally in art's most populist form: the cinema. Jonathan Rutherford remarks that one 'of the nastier fall-out effects of the Thatcher [and Reagan] revolution [is the] glorification of strength and masculinity which comes as a side effect of the culture of success'.[3] This is nowhere more apparent than in Hollywood action cinema, which became obsessively centred upon the body of the action-hero. Through the bodybuilt star, typified by Sylvester Stallone and onetime professional bodybuilder Arnold Schwarzenegger, the muscular body became literally inscribed with the narratives of right-wing ideologies. As Yvonne Tasker observes: 'The pumped-up figure of Stallone seemed to offer more than just a metaphor, functioning for various cultural commentators as the literal embodiment of American interventionism [in Vietnam]'.[4]

From this historical and political contextualisation, I want to make a metaphoric connection between British New Labour and such representations of muscularity. New Labour has received much media and academic attention in being a party that, initially at least, prioritised the need for a strong image above all else. The Government's actual policies, meanwhile, are often described via the discourse of the 'third way', a term suggesting a political base that combines previously antithetical policies (though without, of course, being dialectical!).

---

2. Margaret Walters, *The Male Nude*, Paddington Press, London and New York 1978, p11.
3. J. Rutherford, *Men's Silences: Predicaments in Masculinity*, Routledge, London 1992, p175.
4. Yvonne Tasker, *Spectacular Bodies*, Routledge, London, p92.

Because of this penchant for image and a mix of policies more akin to the American 'party ticket' than to class-based politics, it has been difficult to find any consistent and substantial ideological centre beneath its pachydermal political skin. This is exemplified by the difficulty which various satirists have had in critiquing a party that is, quite simply, a political 'floating signifier'. As Andrew Marr has pointed out: 'That is hardly surprising. If satire is about wrenching apart image and reality, how does it deal with a government whose image is protected so obsessively, and whose hard, inner reality is so difficult to grasp? How do you have a good belly-laugh about the Third Way?'[5]

When New Labour first came to power, Tony Blair spoke of his government's mission to create a 'New Britain'. Throughout the later 1990s, this 'New Britain' has been in evidence particularly in relation to constitutional reform. So, for example, the increasing independence of Scotland, Wales and even Ulster suggests a change that indelibly transforms Britain both politically and socially. The body politic, then, has been *reinvented*, though without actually changing any physical boundaries.

Bodybuilding is equally centred on the possibility of changing the same. The bodybuilder strives to reinvent himself, to create an apparently 'New Body' from the frame of the old. Since the 1950s, bodybuilding adverts have appeared in the back of comic books, appealing to (male) failures and wimps, and offering to transform their body image and *thereby make them successful*. Fitness enthusiasts such as Charles Atlas imbued bodybuilding with the seemingly magical properties of hope, transformation and optimism. The last three elements were certainly present with New Labour's project, from Blair's election as leader to the 1997 election campaign.

New Labour is defined by a marked level of control, its image carefully managed by such figures as Alistair Campbell and Peter Mandelson who operate(d) with clandestine ruthlessness. Thus New Labour is an organisation inhabited by what Michel Foucault would term 'disciplined bodies'. Each New Labour politician is a disciplined body, bound by the very real restrictions that appear to be in place to give the party an image of cohesiveness and unity - a pose - in place of the old ideologies of class. Bodybuilding is also based upon a consummate disposition to discipline, via the careful and ascetic regimentation of exercise and diet, whose outcome is an image - a posed

---

5. Andrew Marr, 'Notice anything Funny?', *The Observer*, 18 October 1998, p1.

simulacrum of power.

In relation to image, then, both New Labour and bodybuilding can be viewed as closely adhering to the codes of 'camp'. Dictionary definitions of camp usually position it as a word that signifies someone (implicitly male) who is effeminate and exaggerates their mannerisms for 'effect'. The problem with such definitions is that camp is a good example of what post-structuralists call 'polysemic plurality'. In other words, camp can mean many things to many people. In some circles, camp refers to an effeminacy of style which seems to produce a not-clandestine homosexuality. In other contexts, camp can be applied to icons such as Judy Garland, Diana Ross, Cher or Bette Midler who were/are known for exaggerated and immoderate performances on the stage and/or screen; or even to the stars of under-acted soaps such as *Coronation Street*.

Camp has often been appropriated by gay culture as means of identification and empowerment. Yet camp need not nor should not be singled down to one area of influence and practice: rock musicians' transgressive dress codes, for example, could, indeed should, be called camp, but can seldom be read as signifying a particular sexual orientation. The genealogy of camp may be seen in relation to the French 'se camper' which means to act in a way that is frail, like a tent. In this sense, flimsiness signifies kitschness, vanity, and theatricality. In the context of this essay, both New Labour and bodybuilding are discourses I would call *unintentionally camp*.

Bodybuilding is camp in that it advocates an *exaggeration of style*. Professional bodybuilders aim to produce what Alan Klein calls 'a comic book masculinity' with body-parts so large and defined that they end up creating an apparent hypermasculinity.[6] With this level of exaggeration, the body is designed to operate without an act: to paraphrase Scott Bukatman, the body's 'presence is its text'.[7] Unlike the Greek tradition on which it is based - where exercised bodies were not only aesthetically pleasing but also designed for warfare - contemporary bodybuilding celebrates muscularity for its own sake. Indeed, many bodybuilders are in effect disabled by the size and weight of their bodies - unable to run, to

---

6. Alan M. Klein, *Little Big Men: Bodybuilding Subculture and Gender Construction*, State University of New York Press, Albany 1993, p234.
7. Scott Bukatman, 'X-Bodies (the torment of the mutant superhero)' in Rodney Sappington and Tyler Stallings (eds), *Uncontrollable Bodies: Testimonies of Identity and Culture*, Bay Press, Seattle 1994, p101.

bend their torsos, in some cases even to bend their arms. The bodybuilder's work-outs operate to generate pure image. The bodybuilt New Labour, likewise, began office as 'pure image', or, to recoin a term from Jean Baudrillard, as *simulacrum* where *image* becomes quite detached from the *real*(ity) - of policy.

The bodybuilt New Labour also expresses the camp characteristic of needing to, in Susan Sontag's words, 'see everything in quotation marks'. By their excessive size and musculature bodybuilders are highlighted as 'men' via the most blatant of gender stereotypes. Similarly, Tony Blair is very self-consciously a 'politician' who knows that his (pose)ition is largely about style and the careful coding of one's image, the delivery of a speech in the appropriate dress, using the appropriate vocabulary, and so on.

New Labour's artifice and style has been nowhere more apparent than with Peter Mandelson. As 'Minister without portfolio' he seemed the perfect New Labourite: quite obviously a politician, but one with no clear, identifiable role. Likewise, when he was given the task of overseeing the Millennium Dome project, the structure itself had no coherent purpose; there was a highly stylised exterior, but no agreed content. With the bodybuilt New Labour, *style*, to paraphrase Jonathan Dollimore, is mistaken 'for the natural' or, in other words, for the *thing itself*. Everything becomes reduced to a question of aesthetics.

Judith Williamson remarked shortly after New Labour came to power how many commentators have pointed out that verbs are almost completely missing from New Labour's key vocabulary: 'it is, on the other hand, chock-a-block with adjectives ("modern", "British", "caring", "tough" etc). As we know, verbs are "doing words" and their absence from Labour language is revealing'.[8] Bodybuilding has often been criticised for being a sport that lacks a purpose behind the muscles and poses, since these bodies do not seem to be used to *do* anything. However, *form* is exactly the purpose: in the distance between manifesto promises and proposed legislation such as the Freedom of Information Bill, we can read the form without content of New Labour's strongly posed, bodybuilt camp.

---

8. *The Guardian*, 14 July 1997, p8.

Education

Today & Tomorrow

Re-Imagining Education - the final issue

Editorial: The End of an Era or the Beginning of the New?
Simon Warren
Education - Past Its Sell-by Date? -
Melian Mansfield
School Britannia
Roland Meighan
Cinderella and the Princess - Adult Education and New Labour
Michael Freeston
Retreat, Renewal or Resistance? The 3 Rs of Teacher Trade Unionism
Stewart Newsam
Goodbye Education - Why *ETT* is going electronic

ETT Online -
From February 2000 *ETT* will provide a complete electronic service :
articles discussing the key political issues in education, providing
international coverage; **debating area** - an open forum for discussing
and critiquing strategy and tactics, as well as an exchange of
campaigning information; and **campaign resources**. This will be a
new political space for critical dialogue between those interested in
democratic and radical education.

For more information contact: Simon Warren, 25 Greenridge Road,
Handsworth Wood, Birmingham, B20 1JL.

ETT Online: www.ett.org.uk

English Imaginaries
Anglo-British Approaches
to Modernity
Kevin Davey

*Recommended retail price £12.99.
Available to Soundings readers for
£10.99 post free.*

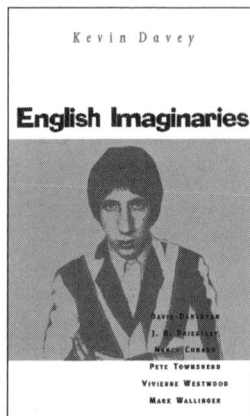

Kevin Davey

English Imaginaries

DAVID DABYDEEN
J. B. PRIESTLEY
NANCY CUNARD
PETE TOWNSHEND
VIVIENNE WESTWOOD
MARK WALLINGER

What does it mean to be English in the modern
world? The answer doesn't usually include Nancy Cunard's assault on
Anglo British whitenes, J. B. Priestley's democratic populism, Who
guitarist Pete Townshend's modernist rebellion, Vivienne Westwood's anti-
fashion, David Dabydeen's blackening of the literary and visual canon or
Mark Wallinger's detourement of English oil painting. Kevin Davey,
drawing on the work of Gramsci and Julia Kristeva, argues that it should
and goes on to ask some searching questions about New Labour's vision
of the nation.

> *'With this book the debate about
> Englishness grows up. In his profound
> meditation Kevin Davey puts to shame
> most of the recent spate of essays on this
> fashionable theme.'* Anthony Barnett

*Please send cheque for £10.99 made out to Lawrence and Wishart
to L&W, 99a Wallis Road London E9 5LN.*

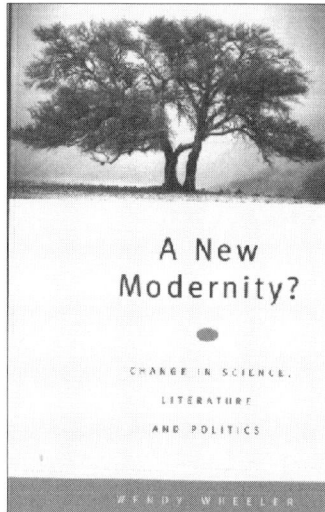

Soundings

Described by the political theorist John Gray as a 'well written and welcome journal', Soundings is a unique venture that combines hard-edged political argument with a broad spectrum of cultural content. Recent highlights have included Stuart Hall, Jackie Kay, Gail Lewis, Mike Phillips and Lola Young on the significance of Windrush; Victoria Brittain and Basil Davidson on states of Africa; Chantal Mouffe on the third way; Angela McRobbie on the culture industries; and Bill Schwarz on the Tories; special themes have also included the European Left, Young Britain, Active Welfare and the Media.

SPECIAL OFFER TO NEW SUBSCRIBERS

First time individual subscribers are entitled to a £25 subscription for the first year

Subscription rates 2000 (3 issues)

Individual subscriptions: UK £35.00 Rest of the World £45
Institutional subscriptions: UK £70.00 Rest of the World £80.00